William L Terhune

My Friend, the Captain; Or, two Yankees in Europe

A Descriptive Story of a Tour of Europe

William L Terhune

My Friend, the Captain; Or, two Yankees in Europe
A Descriptive Story of a Tour of Europe

ISBN/EAN: 9783337076375

Printed in Europe, USA, Canada, Australia, Japan

Cover: Foto ©Andreas Hilbeck / pixelio.de

More available books at **www.hansebooks.com**

My Friend, the Captain;

OR,

TWO YANKEES IN EUROPE.

A Descriptive Story of a Tour of Europe.

WRITTEN AND COMPILED BY
WILLIAM L. TERHUNE.

ILLUSTRATED.

NEW YORK:
G. W. Dillingham Co., Publishers.
MDCCCXCVIII.
[*All rights reserved.*]

COPYRIGHT
1898
BY W. L. TERHUNE.

To My Dear Friend,

CAPT. R. B. GROVER,

who was my companion while touring Europe during the summer of 1897, I affectionately dedicate this book.

My Friend, The Captain.

PREFACE.

The pleasures of a European tour cannot be realized except by actual experience. It has been my good fortune to visit, at different times, the places made famous in history and story, not only in England, Ireland and Scotland, but nearly all of Europe west of the Russian Empire. Since my last tour I have been asked so many questions about different places that, in an unguarded moment, I decided to tell the story in book form.

This account is given in the order the tour was made. It has been my purpose to describe as minutely, yet as briefly as possible, the vast panorama of attractions that passed before me during the four summer months of 1897.

I do not pose as a historian, but repeat some interesting descriptions of places and things which have a record in the past and about which all lovers of history like to read. The descriptions presented here were gathered by me from many sources, and have been written and arranged for the information of the reader and tourist.

To the reader who has visited Europe, this book will be interesting as a reminder of many places and scenes familiar to him or her, some of which have, no doubt, left lasting impressions. To the reader who contemplates a first trip, this will serve as a preparation, while to the reader who never has, and never expects to cross the broad Atlantic, this may serve to show, in a measure, what exists in the Old World.

But, the Captain—my dear friend, the Captain! He is not a myth. He is the best, kindest-hearted and jolliest of living mortals. To him, and to him, alone, I owe the real cause for writing this book. He was my companion, and the life of the four months we spent abroad. Long live the Captain.

W. L. T.

CONTENTS.

	PAGE
CHAPTER I.—Preparing for the Trip, ...	9
CHAPTER II.—How to Do London in Two Weeks, ...	20
CHAPTER III.—Some Things Seen and Heard in London, . .	34
CHAPTER IV.—Doing Quaint Old Holland, ...	47
CHAPTER V.—Antwerp, Brussels and Cologne, ...	59
CHAPTER VI.—A Day on the River Rhine, ...	71
CHAPTER VII.—In Fatherland, ...	87
CHAPTER VIII.—Nuremberg and Munich, ...	102
CHAPTER IX.—Our First Week in Switzerland, ...	118
CHAPTER X.—Adieu to the Land of the Swiss, ...	136
CHAPTER XI.—How to Do Paris, ...	151
CHAPTER XII.—Still Doing Paris, ...	163
CHAPTER XIII.—Versailles and Fontainebleau, ...	176
CHAPTER XIV.—Last Days in the Gay French Capital, . . .	191
CHAPTER XV.—Cambridge and Oxford, ...	201
CHAPTER XVI.—Windsor Castle and Eton College, ...	220
CHAPTER XVII.—Stoke Poges and Hampton Court, ...	235
CHAPTER XVIII.—The Home of Shakespeare, ...	250
CHAPTER XIX.—Chester and Hawarden, ...	262

LIST OF ILLUSTRATIONS

	PAGE
W. L. Terhune	*Frontispiece*
My Friend, the Captain	*Frontispiece*
The Steamer "Majestic," in which we made our trip	14
The Tower of London	22
Scene on High Holborn, London	26
Trafalgar Square, London	30
The Nightingale Tomb in Westminster Abbey, London	36
The Marble Arch, Hyde Park, London	40
The Thames Embankment, London	44
Typical Scene in Holland	48
The Little Palace in the Woods, The Hague	50
On the Beach at Scheveningen, Holland	52
Rokin Canal, Amsterdam	54
Achterburgwal—Old Part of Amsterdam	56
Hotel de Ville, Antwerp, and Statue of Brabo	58
Milk Venders, Antwerp	60
Palace of the Count of Flanders, Brussels	62
King's Palace, Brussels	64
Field of Waterloo, Near Brussels	66
Cathedral at Cologne	68
Old Castle on the Rhine, Near Coblenz	72
Rhinestein Castle, on the Rhine	76
Castle and Fortifications on the Rhine	80
Old Castle on the Rhine, Near Bingen	84
Mosaic Beds in the Palm Garden, Frankfort	88
The Palm Garden, Frankfort	90
The Conservatory, Palm Garden, Frankfort	92
The Old Castle, Heidelberg	94
Students Fencing at Heidelberg	96
Heidelberg University	98
The Great Wine Cask, Heidelberg	100
Maximilian Palace from the River Isra, Nuremberg	104

LIST OF ILLUSTRATIONS.

	PAGE
Five Cornered Tower, Nuremberg	106
Karlsbridge, with St. Sebolds Church, Nuremberg	110
Hangman's Bridge, Nuremberg	112
Ludwigstrasse, Munich	114
The Royal Palace, Munich	116
Zurich from the Lake	120
Lucerne and the Alps	122
The Lion in the Rock, Lucerne	124
Rigi-Kulm Railway, Near Lucerne	126
The Jungfrau from Interlaken	128
The Snow-Clad Jungfrau	130
Staubbach Falls at Lauterbrunnen	132
Brunig Pass and Railway	134
General View of Berne	138
The Bear Pit at Berne	140
Castle of Chillon, Dent-du-Midi in the Distance	142
The Prison in Castle Chillon	144
Chamounix, with a View of Mont Blanc	146
The Captain and His Mule	148
View of Geneva from the **Lake**	150
Notre Dame, Paris	154
Champs Elysees, Paris	156
Avenue de l'Opera, Looking Toward the Opera House, Paris	158
The Trocadero and **Bridge**, Paris	160
Garden of the Tuileries, **Paris**	164
Tomb of Napoleon, **Hotel des Invalides, Paris**	168
Interior of Grand Opera House, Paris	172
The Pantheon, Paris	174
Palace at Versailles, **Near Paris**	178
The Great Fountain at Versailles	182
Palace **at** Fontainebleau, Near Paris	184
Gallery in the **Palace at** Fontainebleau	188
Bois de Boulogne, Paris	194
Room in the Cluny Museum, **Paris**	198
Clare College Bridge, **Cambridge**, England	202
Bridge of Sighs, St. **John's** College, Cambridge, England	206
King's **Gateway**, Entrance to Trinity College, Cambridge, England	208

LIST OF ILLUSTRATIONS.

	PAGE
General View of Oxford, England	210
King's College, Cambridge, England	212
New College, Cloister and Tower, Oxford, England	214
Entrance to Wadham College, Oxford, England	218
Windsor Castle, East Terrace	222
Windsor Castle, Norman Gateway	224
Windsor Castle, North Terrace	228
Windsor Castle, Round Tower	230
Eton College, Eton, England	232
Church and Churchyard, Stoke Poges, England	236
West Front, Wolsey Palace, Hampton Court, England	238
The Great Hall, Hampton Court, England	242
Entrance to Pond Garden, Hampton Court, England	246
Anne Boleyn's Gateway, Hampton Court, England	248
House in Which Shakespeare Was Born, Stratford-on-Avon, England	252
Interior of Holy Trinity Church, Stratford-on-Avon, England	254
Room in Which Shakespeare Was Born, Stratford-on-Avon, England	258
Anne Hathaway's Cottage, Shottery, Near Stratford-on-Avon, England	260
Typical Street View, Chester, England	264
Water Tower and Walls, Chester, England	266
Eaton Hall, Chester, England	270
Rt. Hon. William E. Gladstone	272
Hawarden Castle, the Gladstone Residence	274
"The Keep." Ruins of the Old Castle at Hawarden	276

MY FRIEND, THE CAPTAIN;

OR,

Two Yankees in Europe.

CHAPTER I.

Preparing for the Trip.

IT WAS on a beautiful summer night in August, 1896, that I was seated with a group of gentlemen on the broad piazza of the Deer Park Hotel, North Woodstock, N. H., which is situated at the opening of the Franconia Notch in one of the most beautiful spots of the White Mountain districts. Our conversation had been on Europe, and the members of the party who had been abroad, in which I found myself one of the number, had been entertaining each other with our impressions of the other side. I must admit that some of the experiences related by the members of the party, not including my own, were rather interesting to those who had never crossed the broad Atlantic, but to none more so than my friend, the Captain, who, after hearing an account of a visit to the Palace at Munich, jumped to his feet and remarked:

"I'll wager the best box of cigars I can buy that there is not a member of this company who will guarantee to make a tour of Europe with me next summer."

I immediately accepted the wager.

The Captain was a well known shoe manufacturer. He had commenced in life a poor man, but had built up a great business which brought him prosperity. I had known him for years, and a more jovial or better hearted man did not live in New England. The Captain was original, and would cause more fun to the square inch than anyone I ever knew; therefore, when I accepted his offer, he turned to me and remarked:

"You have toured Europe before?"

"I have."

"You want to go again?"

"I do."

"You're willing to go next year and put in four months?"

"I am."

"Well," concluded the Captain, "if you go I'll give you two boxes of cigars. You are authorized by me to make all the arrangements."

That night I happened to be up later than usual, and from the window of the smoking room where I was sitting I imagined I heard strange talk on the piazza; so glancing through the curtains I found the Captain seated under a gaslight, and in his hands he had a little book which he was deeply interested in, and from which he was quoting, something like this:

"*Parlez—Parlez—Parlez vous—Parlez vous Francaise?*"

I became interested and, walking out on the piazza, approached the Captain and asked him what he was doing.

"I am studying up French," was the only reply he made, as he again glanced at his book. This was enough for me, and I left the Captain to enjoy the work he had entered on.

So, by the Captain's order, I commenced preparations for our trip, and early the next March I engaged accommodations on that magnificent steamship, the Majestic, sailing from New York on Wednesday, June 2.

Little did I know what was in store for me in the weeks and months to come. I loved travel, and I was looking forward to the time when I would have the Captain as a companion, little dreaming that the Captain was to start on this trip with the intention of seeing and knowing the country, regardless of all consequences.

Leaving New York per steamship Majestic, we sailed down the harbor on a beautiful June day, and when the shades of night fell over us we were far from sight of land in a calm, peaceful sea. The trip was made without "inconvenience" to our party, yet the Captain insists he never saw a worse specimen of humanity than he beheld in the writer on the Sunday morning after our departure; but this I brand as false. The Captain was not responsible for what he saw that morning, and I was.

In preparing for a European trip one must bear in mind that the weather on the other side is variable, consequently he must travel with both heavy and light clothing, including a suit for steamer wear that must be heavy, one that has seen service will answer the purpose. Passports are not obligatory, but it is advisable to be provided with one. It is useful as a means of identification, viewing public buildings, etc.

The arrangements for money while abroad can be easily adjusted. If one is traveling considerably a Letter of Credit for anything over $500 is preferable, and for smaller sums American Express money orders answer the same purpose. For a residence of some weeks in a city, your letter of credit will answer the purpose. A small amount of English, French and German currency should be carried for use on the respective steamers and on landing in the countries.

A steamer trunk to take in your stateroom is a necessity, and must not be over fourteen or fifteen inches deep. This must be marked with the number of your room or it will go in the hold. After the steamer leaves the dock you must apply to the second steward in the dining room, who will allot you your seat at the table. Every steamer has an experienced surgeon on board, and in case you use his services a reasonable fee is expected. The other fees required are as follows: Bedroom and table steward, ten shillings or $2.50. "Boots," two and six or sixty cents, and the deck steward about three shillings, seventy-five cents, while a small fee of two shillings, fifty cents, is usually given the smoke room and the toilet room steward. There is always a good barber, who will give you a shave for a shilling, twenty-five cents.

Our departure from New York on our trip outward was made at 12 o'clock, and at 1.30 lunch was served. When the signal was given the Captain approached me and remarked that he was rather anxious to go to the dining room. Supposing he was in good condition for a hearty meal, I accompanied him and sat down beside him. Taking up the bill of fare, the Captain looked at it for a moment and threw it down in disgust.

"What is the matter, Captain?" I asked.

"Why," was his reply, "I thought we were going to have a table dee hotey dinner."

"We have a table d'hote at 6.30 tonight," was my reply.

"Well," **returned the Captain,** "that may suit you and the rest of these foreigners, **but so far as I am** concerned, **when it** comes night-time I want my tea."

Nearly all the modern steamers are fitted with a library, containing all that is choice in biography, novel or fiction. The books **are** in charge of a steward, who delivers them to the passengers, taking a receipt therefor, to be returned before the end of the voyage.

The points of the compass may be determined by the aid of an ordinary watch. It is simply necessary to bring the watch in a position so that **the hour** hand is directed toward the sun. The south then lies exactly midway between whatever hour it may happen to be and the **numeral XII. on** the dial. Let us suppose, **for** instance, that **it is 4 o'clock, and** that the time-piece is **held in the position indicated. The direction of the** numeral II. will then be the exact south. **If it is 8 o'clock the numeral X. will indicate the exact** southerly **point.**

In the matter **of** railroad traveling there are, in most countries, **three** classes of carriages. The first-class is usually furnished with plush; second-class carriages are furnished almost as well. Second-class in Germany is as comfortable as first-class in England, France and Italy; and this is so well understood, that mixed tickets **are** sold for long journeys entitling the holder to first-class in other countries and second-class in Germany. In England third-class coaches are comfortable. This class is frequented by the general public for short journeys. Nearly every train has compartments **exclusively** for ladies. In England, **France and** Italy, smoking is forbidden, except in **compartments specially** designated for that purpose.

The allowance of baggage or luggage differs. In England it is one hundred pounds; **in** most continental countries it averages fifty pounds; in Bavaria, Belgium, Italy, and in most parts of Switzerland there is no allowance. The charge for excessive luggage is high; **all** hand baggage is free. **The system of** checking baggage is unknown abroad.

The most desirable seasons for visiting the various resorts **of** Europe are well known to **the** old traveler, but the methods for reaching them are continually improving. The new Mediterranean service, which has become so popular **for winter** travel, has made **a direct communication between the United States** and Spain, Italy and Egypt. These trips make a pleasant vacation of six weeks during the winter season and include all points of interest in the Mediterranean countries. The North Cape and Land of the Midnight Sun has also been brought in direct communication with the United States by special excursion steamers sailing in June and July, and touching all ports of interest in Norway and Sweden. Switzerland, reached via France or Germany, is visited principally during June, July, August and September. The London season is at its height in May and June, and Scotland is sought for its shooting in the fall of the year. Paris has no stated season for travelers, all months being popular at this capital. The latter points are reached directly by steamers; London via Liverpool and Southampton; Scotland via Glasgow and Edinburgh; and Paris via Havre, Coulogne sur-Mer and Antwerp.

It is the custom in England and among the English servants and others to speak of their superior or employer as the "Guv'nor," the same as we speak of such as the "Boss." The second day out from New York, the Captain and I were enjoying a cigar in the smoking room, after our dinner, when the steward approached us and addressing the Captain, remarked:

"Guv'nor, will you have some coffee?"

The Captain dropped his cigar on the floor and stared at the man for an instant, and after the steward had supplied him with his coffee and passed on, the Captain nudged me and in great glee remarked:

"Did you hear that?"

"Hear what?" I remarked.

"Why, that fellow takes me for the Governor of Massachusetts," and then the Captain leaned back in his easy chair and smoked three cigars before retiring to his state-room.

The following is a table showing the value of English money in American coin:

GOLD.		SILVER.	
One sovereign,	$4.86	Crown, 5s.,	$1.20
One-half sovereign,	2.43	One-half crown, 2s. 6d.,	.60
		One florin, 2s.,	.48
BANK NOTES.		One shilling,	.24
		Six pence,	.12
£5 Bank of England,	24.30	Four pence,	.08
£1 Irish and Scotch,	4.86	Three pence,	.06

The Steamer "Majestic," in which we made our trip.

Here is a table of French money :

5 centimes, 1 sou,	equal to $ .01
50 centimes, 10 sous—one-half franc,	" .10
100 centimes, 20 sous—one franc,	" .20
5 franc piece, gold or silver,	" 1.00
10 franc piece, gold or silver,	" 2.00
20 franc piece, gold or silver,	" 4.00

German money is Americanized as follows :

5 pfennigs,	equal to $ .01
10 pfennigs,	" .02
20 pfennigs,	" .05
50 pfennigs or one-half mark,	" .12
1 mark,	" .23
3 marks or 1 thaler,	" .69
10 marks,	" 2.37
20 marks,	" 4.74

Cab fares in Europe are low. The following are the rates charged in London :

BY DISTANCE—Hansom or "four wheeler," the same. First two miles, 1s.; for every additional mile, 6d. For each fifteen minutes' waiting en route, 6d.

BY TIME—Hansom (two-wheeler) 2s., 6d. per hour. Cab (four-wheeler), 2s. per hour.

EXTRA—Each article of baggage outside, 2d. additional. More than two persons, 6d. each additional.

Paris rates are as follows :

VOITURES DE PLACE—Hired in the street.
PER COURSE—Any distance inside the gates.

Two-seated voiture, per course,	1 franc, 50 centimes,	$.30
Four-seated voiture, per course,	2 francs,	.40

PER HOUR.

Two-seated voiture, by the hour,	2 francs,	$.40
Four-seated voiture, by the hour,	2 francs, 50 centimes,	.50

We are supposed to speak the same language as our English cousins. This to a great extent is true, but it is also true that those proud and patriotic citizens who believe that they speak "United States" have some amount of reason for their belief. It is certainly a fact that many important differences now exist between the

English spoken in America and the English spoken in the United Kingdom. These differences in phraseology are oftentimes the cause of much trouble and annoyance to American travelers, because many terms which are peculiarly American are unknown to the average Englishman. A common experience, by way of illustration, is that of the American who wanders about the streets of London, inquiring the way to the nearest "railroad depot," and usually fails to find the object of his search. What he wants, of course, is the "railway station." It is also an everyday experience for American ladies to enter English shops and ask for articles of merchandise which, to their surprise, they find are things unheard of. The trouble is that they employ the American instead of the English descriptive titles and these are not generally known. These might be illustrated extensively, but enough has been said to show that a vast amount of inconvenience may be avoided by the American traveler who has placed at his disposal a list of these puzzling differences in language, in order that he may know how to speak English so as to be understood by English people of every class. It is with this object in view that the following list of varying familiar phrases has been compiled:

AMERICAN.	ENGLISH.
The railroad.	The railway.
The station agent.	The station master.
The telegraph operator.	The telegraph clerk, (pronounced "clark").
The sleeper.	The Pullman.
The depot.	The railway station.
The smoking car.	The smoking carriage.
The cars or train.	The carriages or train.
The ticket office.	The booking office.
The section of a car.	The compartment of a carriage.
Changing cars.	Changing carriages.
The conductor.	The guard.
The locomotive engineer.	The engine driver.
The track.	The line.
The switch.	The points.
The switchman.	The pointsman.
The brakeman.	The porter.
The elevated railroad.	The overhead railway.
Checking baggage.	Registering luggage.
The baggage.	The luggage.

The baggage room.	The luggage booking-office.
The trunk.	(Sometimes) the box.
The valise, satchel or "grip."	The bag or portmanteau.
Cloak-room or parcel office.	Left-luggage office or cloak-room.
The hack.	The cab.
The street car.	The tram or tramway.
A buggy or light carriage.	A trap.

Such well-known American dishes as pork and beans, fishballs, American pies, cookies, crullers, buckwheat cakes, and sweet corn can be obtained at only a few restaurants in London. In nearly all restaurants these Yankee dishes are almost unknown. It should also be added that barley, wheat, etc., in England, are often referred to as "corn," while corn, in the American sense, is always spoken of as "Indian corn," or "maize," and can be obtained only in the dried state.

In Europe, "dessert" applies to only the fruit portion of the menu. Pudding and other dishes of the kind are referred to as "sweets." The word "pastry" refers to all kinds of cakes, puffs, tarts, etc. A visit to Low's Exchange on Northumberland avenue will be of benefit to all American tourists.

The American pie is unknown in Europe, but the Captain did not know this. The day before our arrival at Liverpool, after finishing his dinner, the Captain called his dining-room steward and addressing him as "waiter," ordered a piece of pie. The steward looked at him for a moment and replied :

"Pie, pie, what kind of pie, sir?"

The Captain's reply was that "Apple would do," but he was rather taken back when the steward informed him that there was only ham or meat pie. Consequently I had to explain to him the situation of affairs, and after I had explained it to him the Captain turned to me and remarked :

"No pies in Europe ! What a blasted country it must be."

Although the Captain got the English phrase "blasted" he did not get his American pie.

AMERICAN.	ENGLISH.
A list of charges at restaurants or hotels.	A tariff.
Tenderloin steak.	Fillet steak.
Round steak.	Buttock steak.
First cut of the roast.	Wing rib.
A chicken.	A fowl.

Squash. Vegetable marrow.
Lima beans. Broad beans.
Pulverized **sugar**. Icing sugar.
String beans. French beans.

ON THE STREET.   IN THE STREET.

The **sidewalk**. The pavement.
A block. A turning.

The word "**block**" is not used in England to designate distance. An American would say, "**About** four blocks from here." An Englishman **would say**, "**The fourth** turning from here," when directing a person.

AMERICAN.   ENGLISH.

Shoes (ladies' or gentlemen's). Boots.
Men's high boots. Top boots.
Half or low shoes. Shoes.
Gaiters. Elastic-side **boots**.
Rubbers. Goloshes.
A Prince Albert. A frock coat.
A cut-away. A morning coat.
A vest. A waistcoat.
Leggins. Gaiters.
A Derby hat. A felt hat or "bowler."

Names of stores and merchandise:

AMERICAN.   ENGLISH.

Dress waist. Body or bodice.
A store. A shop.
A notion store. A haberdasher's.
Notions. Haberdashery.
A drug store. A chemist's.
A candy store. A confectioner's or sweet shop.
Candy or bon-bons. Sweets.
A clerk or salesman. A shopman.
A saleslady. A shop girl.
A floor walker. A shop walker.
The dry goods store. The linen draper's shop.
A spool of thread. A reel of cotton.
India **muslin**. Book muslin.
Muslin. Calico **or long cloth**.
Calico. Print.
A veil. A veil or fall.
Swiss. Muslin.

The foregoing may be rather uninteresting to most of the readers of this book, but there may be some points of interest for those who are contemplating a first trip to Europe.

Here is a little incident I almost forgot to mention. Immediately upon arrival in Liverpool I noticed the Captain was very anxious to be one of the first to go down the gang plank. I followed closely after, and on reaching the landing stage found the Captain busily writing a telegram at the telegraph office. Glancing over his shoulders, I was surprised to read the following:

          LIVERPOOL, June 9, 1897.
PRINCE OF WALES, Marlborough House, London:
 Just arrived. Will stop at the Langham.
     (Signed) THE CAPTAIN.

Hardly knowing whether I was in Liverpool or New York, I asked the Captain what his intention was in writing such a telegram.

"Why," was his reply, "I am going to send it to the Prince of Wales."

"For what reason?" I asked.

"To let him know we have arrived," was his reply. "If there is anything going on in London we want to be in it, and if there is any man that can help us, it is the Prince."

The last I saw of the Captain he was paying 9d. for the telegram and I was contemplating whether to go back to the United States or continue my trip.

CHAPTER II.

How To Do London in Two Weeks.

A FEW days after my arrival in London I received a letter from one of my friends in Boston, in which he asked me how I got along with the Captain, and if I was fully satisfied with him as a traveling companion. It brought to my mind an old story which I heard years ago, of a German whose wife had died. Shortly after the last sad rites, Hans met a friend on the street, who condoled with him and asked if his wife was resigned.

"Vot's dat?" said Hans.

"Was your wife resigned?"

"Resigned, resigned, mine Gott, she had to pe!"

So with myself, I had no choice. I had to be.

Take my advice and go to Europe, if you have to go over in the steerage. Why? Because you will return to your homes better and more patriotic citizens. Better, because you will realize that you live in the greatest country upon which the sun shines. More patriotic, because you will get an additional strain in that direction here. Englishmen are all patriotic. I am glad to see it, and yet I met many who were almost as loud in their praise of America as a native would have been.

It is quite a feat to do London and do it thoroughly in a short space of time, therefore it is my purpose to tell you how much of London one might see in a two weeks' stay there.

First, on arriving in London, there are three things to remember. The average cost for three meals and bedroom at a first-class hotel is $4 to $5 per day; hotel accommodations can be secured as low as $2.50 to $3 per day, but they are not generally satisfactory to one who is particular and used to good living. Pensions or boarding houses are to be found in all sections. Good accommodations can be secured from $7.50 to $10 per week, including room, breakfast and dinner. Restaurants abound wherever you go. In fact, there are more restaurants, cigar, hair and jewelry stores than any other lines. A first-class restaurant is as expensive as the same class in New York, Boston, or any other of our large cities. For instance, a cup of tea or coffee costs from twelve to twenty-five cents, a dozen raw oysters from fifty cents to $1, and every other item in like proportion.

The shops or stores of London, Paris, or any other of the continental cities will not compare for elegance and fine window displays with those of the large American cities. A cab can be hired to carry one or two persons any reasonable distance (two miles is the limit) for twenty-five cents for the two. Buses or stages are the most popular for city transit. One advantage they possess is the seating capacity on top, where a fine view can be had during the trip. Prices vary from two cents upward per ride. To a person going a short distance this is an advantage, but for a three, four or five-mile ride they are more expensive then our electric cars. A good seat at the theater costs $2.50. An ordinary telegram costs twelve cents.

The day after we arrived in London we took a ride down town, got off at the Bank of England, and were strolling along, when the Captain nudged me as we came to a street corner. "Step around here," was all he said. Not knowing what was coming I obeyed, and as soon as the street was clear, the captain looked at me, and asking me to "join in the chorus," started off with the "Star Spangled Banner." After considerable effort I got him to move on.

Now let me outline a two weeks' stay in London, supposing one does not care to do it with a rush, but see the principal sights and at the same time enjoy a restful period between.

First Day—We will suppose you are at the West End. Take a bus at Oxford circus, secure a seat on top and go down Regent street, passing many of the best stores, to Piccadilly circus (a circus is a square), thence to Trafalgar square. Here in the center is the monument erected to Nelson, on the left is the National Art Gallery and St. Martin's Church ; to the right is Whitehall street, leading to the Horse Guards, Westminster Abbey and the Houses of Parliament, also Northumberland avenue leading to Victoria embankment, and containing the three great hotels—the Metropole, Victoria and Grand. From here we pass down the Strand. On the left below the square is the Charing Cross station, and further down the division line between old London and the new. On the left, as you come to

The Tower of London.

Chancery lane, is the Law Courts, or Court House, and then the Strand is continued as Fleet street, the "newspaper row" of London. From Fleet street you pass to Ludgate circus, off which is Blackfriar's bridge; thence through Ludgate Hill, passing St. Paul's, through Cannon street to Queen street and Poultry, where stands the Mansion House, the home of the Lord Mayor, and opposite the Bank of England and the Royal Exchange. The tour can be continued through Whitechapel, the poor district of London, and the scene of "Jack the Ripper's" outrages. Returning, you pass through Cheapside, on which is located Bow Church, from whence ring Bow-bells. It is said that all persons who are born within the sound of Bow-bells are Cockneys, or true Londoners.

Off Cheapside is the Guild Hall, and as you pass out of this street you go through Newgate, passing the general post office and Newgate Prison, with Old Bailey on the left. This was once the principal prison of London, and in its day such famous men as William Penn, Daniel Defoe and Jack Sheppard were confined within its walls. Criminals condemned to death are still hanged here. Newgate was built in 1780. At 68 Old Bailey was the former home of Jonathan Wild. Passing from Newgate you go through Holborn Viaduct, where is located Dr. Parker's church, and then pass into New Oxford and Oxford street, through a busy shipping center, to your place of departure. Such a trip will consume one morning, and the afternoon can be spent in one of the many parks.

At the hotel where we stopped in the early part of June were some of the finest strawberries I ever saw. They were not served as a dessert the first day, so when we were finishing our lunch the second day the captain called the waiter and told him to bring on some strawberries. The servant disappeared and soon returned with a small dish with possibly half a dozen berries on it. The captain gazed at it carefully, looked at the waiter and remarked that "the samples are all right; bring on the dish." The waiter departed, and after a consultation with the head waiter, the dish was placed before us, and we enjoyed the berries. When the captain received his bill that week there appeared this item:

"Dessert, £1."

"What's this?" asked the Captain of the clerk.

"Strawberries, sir?" was the answer.

Five dollars was rather a high price for three pints of strawberries but the Captain did not know that we were ahead of the season in London, and these came from the south of France.

Second Day—Take a bus and go down to Whitehall street, visit the Horse Guards and the home of the commander-in-chief of the army, built in 1753. Two mounted Life Guards are posted as sentinels in front, each day from 10 A. M. to 4 P. M., and the operation of relieving the guard, which takes place hourly, is interesting. A parade takes place on the grounds each afternoon about 4 o'clock. From here pass on to the Houses of Parliament (open free on Saturdays, 10 to 4), which cover an area of 8 acres, and contain 11 courts, 100 staircases, and 1100 apartments. The cost was $15,000,000, and the building was erected in 1840. The clock tower is 318 feet high. The large clock has four dials, each 23 feet in diameter, and it takes five hours to wind up the striking parts.

On entering, you pass through the Norman arch to the Queen's robing room, thence through the royal galleries, the Prince's chamber, to the House of Peers. From here you go through the Peers' Lobby and a corridor to the Central Hall, where you again pass through a corridor to the Commons' Lobby, and thence to the House of Commons, returning to the Central Hall, and out by the way of St. Stephen's Hall and Westminster Hall. From the latter you enter the crypt or chapel. A detailed description of this building, with its pictures and artistic constructions would easily fill half a book the size of this.

From the Houses of Parliament pass across the street and you are at Westminster Abbey. The history of this church dates back to 616, but the regular establishment of the Abbey was due to Edward the Confessor, who built a church almost as large as the present one in 1049. The present building was entirely rebuilt by Henry III. and his son, Edward I., in the latter half of the thirteenth century. I wish that I might have time and space to describe this interesting place, but even then I could not do it justice. One must certainly visit it to realize its magnificence. Here are buried Edward the Confessor, Queen Eleanor (his first wife), Henry III., Edward III., Richard II., Edward I., Henry VII., George II., Queen Elizabeth, Edward V., Charles II., William III., Queen Mary and Queen Anne, kings and queens galore, besides their families, men and women noted in the past history of England, and royalty in all its glory.

Among the most striking monuments is one in the chapels of St. John the Evangelist, St. Michael and St. Andrew, formerly three separate chapels, but now combined. Here is a marble group by Roubillac in memory of Lady Nightingale, erected by her husband in 1731, and at his death, 1752, he was buried here. The representation is that of Lady Nightingale, resting on her husband's arm, and in the last hours of her life. Death appears from the tomb, and is launching his dart at the dying lady, while her husband tries to ward off the attack.

> Life is a jest, and all things show it,
> I thought so once, and now I know it.
> —*Gay.*

Third Day—An interesting day may be spent by going to either Westminster Pier or Charing Cross Pier at the foot of Northumberland avenue, and take a boat down the Thames to London bridge; fare two cents. You pass under all the celebrated bridges that cross the river, and have a fine view of the Victoria Embankment, Hotel Cecil and other prominent buildings. Leaving the boat at London bridge you pass under a series of arches to Billingsgate, the great fish center of London, and well worth a visit.

Just beyond is the Tower of London, the ancient fortress and, historically, the most interesting spot in England. This building originated with William the Conqueror, in 1078, and was erected for a royal palace. Here are to be seen the quaintly attired warders, or beef-eaters, styled "Yeomen of the Guard." It may be interesting to know that Prince James of Scotland was imprisoned here in 1405, and it was under the staircase, passing through the wall of the White Tower that the bones of the two young princes, murdered by their uncle, the Duke of Gloucester, afterward Richard III., were found. On the first floor are the apartments in which Sir Walter Raleigh was confined when he wrote his "History of the World." Lady Jane Grey was confined here, and Henry VI. was murdered in Record Tower. Other notables were also confined here, among them being William Wallace, the Scottish chief, and the Duke of Orleans, father of Louis XII,, of France. In the courtyard is the spot where many notables were executed, such as Queen Anne Boleyn, Queen Catherine Howard, Lady Jane Grey and others. The tower is a complete museum of antiques, armor, etc., of every kind and description. Here is also to be seen the crown jewels valued at $75,000,000.

Scene on High Holborn, London.

From our arrival in London to the present time the Captain had not been fully pleased with his menu. "If I only had a good plate of Boston baked beans and a piece of apple pie, I would be fixed," was his exclamation day in and day out.

Fourth Day—Take a bus and go to St. Paul's, the third largest church in the world, its only rivals being the cathedrals at Rome and Milan. The present church was commenced in 1675, first opened for service in 1697, and completed in 1710. It may be interesting to know that this great structure was designed by one man, Sir Christopher Wren, and built by one master mason, Thomas Strong. The cost of the edifice was about $20,000,000, and was defrayed almost wholly by a tax on coal. The architect received a salary of only $5000 per year.

The church somewhat resembles St. Peter's at Rome. It is so hemmed in with narrow streets and large buildings that its proportions cannot be realized. It is 500 feet long and 118 feet wide. The inner dome is 225 feet, and the outer 364 feet from the pavement to the cross. The diameter of the dome is about 112 feet. Here are to be found monuments erected to the illustrious dead of England. To visit London and miss St. Paul's would be like going to a theatre and not seeing the play.

From St. Paul's pass along the left and you are shortly in front of the Mansion House, the official residence of the Lord Mayor of London during the term of his office. This was erected in 1739. Not open to the public. Opposite the Mansion House is the Bank of England, the most powerful financial institution in the world, known as "The Old Lady of Thread-Needle street," as it is located on that thoroughfare. The bank was founded in 1691 by William Paterson, a Scotchman, and is the first joint stock bank established in England, and continued as such until 1834. It is still the only bank in England having the power to issue paper money. Its original capital was $30,000,000, which has increased to nearly $500,000,000. It employs 900 persons, with an annual payroll of over $5,000,000. England pays the bank $5,000,000 per year for managing its national debt, now amounting to $15,500,000,000. It is said that the average amount of money negotiated in the bank per day amounts to $50,000,000. The bank contains a general printing office where it does all its work, including the printing of its bills, some 15,000 daily. A bill is **never issued a** second time; no matter if only a day old the moment they are returned to the bank or **any** of its branches they are condemned.

Passing from the bank to **the end of** King **street is** Guild Hall, or the council room of old **London.** This building is **well** worth inspection. Connected with it is an excellent art gallery and a museum of relics of old London.

Fifth Day—A most instructive and certainly a pleasant half day **can be** profitably passed at the **National** Gallery, Trafalgar square, **the** leading art gallery of England, **which** was erected in 1832 at a **cost of $2,500,000.** It is **460** feet **long,** and contains twenty-two **rooms replete with** works of art by not only **the** most famous old **masters, but** men and women noted in later days.

Sixth Day—**On Great Russell street, off** Oxford street, is located **the** British Museum. **Weeks could be spent** in examining the many curiosities contained therein. **It is** estimated **that** 750,000 people visit this building annually. **Here is to be** found the largest library in the world, containing 80,000 volumes, with over 1,000,000 volumes in reserve. This, however, is only a small part of the great treat **in** store for the sight-seer. Manuscripts and autograph letters of kings and queens long since **dead, and curious** specimens of Nature's and man's handiwork from all parts of the globe. If **possible,** try and arrange **to put** in a full day here.

The manager of the hotel where we **were** located in **London was giving us a** glowing account of the great **naval review in** honor of **the Queen's** Diamond Jubilee, and asked **the Captain if he** was present **to witness it.**

"**No,**" was his **reply; "I can** go to New York any day and **witness as fine** a show from the top **of any** of our tall buildings."

Seventh Day—Soane's **Museum,** founded and owned by Sir John **Soane,** the architect of the Bank of England, is located at 13 Lincoln's Inn Fields, just off Chancery lane or Holburn. It is an interesting place to visit. **Here** is to be found **Hogarth**'s celebrated series of eight pictures illustrating " The Rake's Progress," originally purchased for about $14,000 and now considered priceless. Also by the same artist four pictures illustrating an English election in early **days. In addition to the above there is a large collection** of drawings **by Sir John, as well as numerous curiosities and** bric-a-brac collected by him. This place can be easily visited during the morning, and after lunch, make arrangements to spend the afternoon at Hyde Park, arriving there by 3:30 P. M., and view the magnificent procession of carriages that appear about 4 P. M., a sight well worth seeing and only equaled by the Champs Elysees, Paris, during the Grand Prix in June. If you prefer to take a carriage and start out an hour earlier, you will find in proximity to Hyde Park Buckingham Palace, the Queen's residence when in town, Marlborough House, the residence of the Prince of Wales, St. James' Palace, former residence of the Queen, Kensington Palace, the birthplace of the Queen, York House, etc.

The main entrance to Hyde Park is through the marble arch, originally erected by George IV. at the entrance to Buckingham Palace, at a cost of $400,000. In 1850 it was removed from the Palace, and a year later erected as above. In the afternoon's drive are to be seen the finest turnouts in London, elegant equipages, high bred horses and handsome trappings, with drivers and footmen in showy costume. If perchance you take this in and happen to see a turnout with the coachman and footman in red livery, it is a part of the Royalty, for they alone are allowed to dress their servants in this color.

We were returning from the lower part of London one day, seated on top of a bus, and both of us enjoying our cigars. The Captain occasionally spat over the side of the bus.

"Don't let them catch you doing that, Captain," I said.

"Why?" he remarked.

"Because you will be fined two pounds."

"Fined and be hanged! What do I care?" answered the Captain. "I've got money to burn, and just as lief burn it here as anywhere."

Eighth Day—Go out to Regent Park and visit the Zoological and the Botanical Gardens, two of the most interesting places for a day out in the sunshine in London. One can profitably spend a whole day in these delightful spots.

Ninth Day—When I was last in London I neglected to visit the Crystal Palace. Everybody I met upon my return said, "Oh!" and "Why did you miss it?" etc. This time I went and it was a fête day, too. I got back as quickly as I could, and a more disgusted

Trafalgar Square, London.

party than ours I never met. Take my advice and keep away from the Crystal Palace. It is a dirty, bad-smelling, overgrown barn. If it was located in New York or Boston it would be condemned by the authorities. The show of goods is a poor one and nothing to attract. This much I will say, the building is an imposing one from the exterior and the grounds about it are finely laid out. The building was constructed in 1854 and is 1608 feet long. It was built in eighteen weeks, employing from 4000 to 7000 hands per day in its construction. It is built of glass and iron. But you don't want to waste your time going out there, for it will spoil a whole day of your London visit.

In place of the Crystal Palace, let me suggest you pass a day at Earls Court, more especially if there is an exhibition there. This delightful place can be reached by bus or underground railway or by boat on the Thames. It is beautifully laid out and a most charming place for a day's outing.

Tenth Day—The Kew Gardens are at Kew, a pleasant ride by boat on the Thames. Let me suggest that you start early for Kew and take a view of this beautiful park, then take the tram cars and stage for Hampton Court, where you are due about noon. Here one finds the old palace built by Cardinal Wolsey, afterwards the home of Henry VIII., and later occupied by Cromwell, the Stuarts, William III., and the first two monarchs of the house of Hanover. Since the days of George II. Hampton Court has ceased to be a royal residence. In this old palace is to be found among the numerous interesting rooms the king's first presence chamber, the king's drawing room, bedroom of King William III., which contains the bed of Queen Charlotte. There is a clock in this room that when wound up will go for a year, yet, while in good order, is no longer wound. The queen's bedroom contains Queen Anne's bed. Here are also the rooms of the then Prince of Wales, besides a large number of an interesting nature, seventeen in all, but I cannot tell all about it here; further on I will give you more details and show some illustrations. Leaving Hampton Court, take the boat for London, and if you do not say the ride down is a most charming one, I will agree I am no authority in this direction. To describe a three hours' sail down the Thames is beyond my power. The boats are flat, side wheel, and will carry, say 100 or about that. During the summer, a "band," consisting of a melodeon, a cornet and a flute, "discourse sweet music" and are paid by a collection.

A fine orchestra discoursed sweet music in the corridor of our hotel at London from 6 to 9 P. M. Twice a week it would close the selection with "God Save the Queen," when those present would rise. The first time this occurred after our arrival, the Captain commenced to sing "My Country, 'tis of Thee." I nudged him to keep quiet. "Let me alone," was his response. "They're playing the tune and I am going to sing it."

Eleventh Day—Let me suggest that a visit be made to the Victoria Embankment. This was built from 1864 to 1870 at a cost of $75,000,-000, the amount being raised by taxes levied on coal and wines. The roadway is about 100 feet wide, and extends from Blackfriars to Westminster bridge. While here a visit can be made to the elegant new Hotel Cecil, which faces on the embankment, and is a marvel in hoteldom.

The balance of the day can be employed in a trip to Kensington Gardens, a beautiful spot adjoining Hyde Park, and here is located the Albert Memorial, erected by the queen in memory of her husband, the Prince Consort. Directly opposite is the Royal Albert Hall, built in amphitheater shape, 810 feet in circumference, with a seating capacity of 8000. Fine concerts are given here every Sunday afternoon at 3.30, with seats at twelve cents and twenty-five cents each. The poorest seat in the house commands a full view of the stage.

Twelfth Day—A visit to the South Kensington Museum will surely repay the tourist. Here is to be found a fine collection of exhibits in a gallery of art. Also the Indian Museum close by filled with an exhibit of barbaric curiosities and historic relics, and the Natural History Museum close by, which, as its name implies, is made up of a collection of zoology, geology, mineralogy and botany. All well worth a visit.

This completes the twelve working days in London. One Sunday let me suggest attending services at Westminster, and the other at Dr. Parker's City Temple, Holborn Viaduct. If you can only visit one of the above take in Dr. Parker's, by all means. Dr. Parker is an Englishman by birth, but an intense lover of America and Americans. It may be remembered that after the death of Henry Ward Beecher he was called as pastor of his church, but did not feel as though he could leave his London charge. Every Sunday morning after his prayer for the Queen, he prays for the President of the United States and his people. Services of one hour's duration, from 12 to 1, are held every Thursday noon. I attended one of these. It was the second day after the Queen's Diamond Jubilee, and Dr. Parker announced that he would speak on his impressions of that occasion. The great house was filled; such a dramatic speaker I never before heard in a pulpit. "Soldiers, guns, bayonets, swords, cannons and lances" was his theme, against "Peace, happiness and prosperity." Two little girls about twelve years of age occupied front seats in the choir. When the sermon was ended they sang "God Save the Queen," the audience joining in the last verse, after which Dr. Parker announced they were two little American girls from across the sea, who were in London on a visit, "and now," he concluded, "let us pray for that great country and great people of America."

And he prayed.

As my friend the Captain remarked, "He prayed like a soldier."

While we were in London the Captain and myself visited the Gaiety Theater. It so happened that on the evening in question we occupied a box. After the conclusion of the first act a waiter appeared on the scene with a tray covered with ices, cake, etc., and the Captain ate heartily. After finishing the repast he turned to me and remarked:

"I tell you what, these Englishmen know how to do up things in good shape. Just see how they treat their patrons! Did you ever hear of an American theater manager doing this thing?"

I acknowledged that I had not, but at the conclusion of the second act the Captain was taken aback by the waiter entering and presenting him with a bill for 4s., or $1 United States currency. The Captain paid the bill without a murmur, but he had nothing further to say about the generosity of the English theatrical manager.

CHAPTER III.

Some Things Seen and Heard in London.

DURING the early part of our travels, the Captain delighted to introduce me as "a live Yankee," but an event occurred later on that gave me a new title. We were stopping for a few days at an interior town, and experienced considerable trouble in having our wants carefully looked after.

"If you promise to keep quiet for an hour, I will see we are well cared for," said the Captain, addressing me.

I promised.

That noon at lunch, the same old cause for complaint occurred. The Captain got up from the table, went out where the waiter was finally located, and addressing her, said :

"Do you know who that gentleman is with me?"

"No sir," was the reply.

"Well," said the Captain, "he is the Crown Prince of America, and I advise you to be more careful in your attention to him."

The girl almost fainted, and I was as much surprised as the waiter, when the Captain returned to the table, she following, and bowing and scraping, addressed me as "Your Royal Highness,' and informed me that whatever I wanted I could have. After her departure, the Captain explained the situation. I looked for my hat to beat a hasty departure, and since then the Captain has called me Crown Prince of America. He insists, however, that it is an actual fact, as we are all crown princes in the United States. I guess he is right, although we do not realize this ourselves, yet the Captain declares I walked "stiffer" than I ever did before.

I am going to devote this chapter to minor matters that attracted my attention while in London, the first of which was a series of articles contributed to a London daily paper by Julian Ralph, an American journalist, who put in an appearance in London while I was there. His articles were published under the title of 'As Seen Through

American Eyes." His first was on the beggar question, and he started off by offering an apology to the British public for what he had said in certain letters he, as a newspaper correspondent, wrote to the American press, when he was last in London. It appears in these letters he told the story of the London beggar, and I have no doubt he told it truthfully, but as he had now secured an opportunity to write for the English press the first thing he did was to take it all back and say he had been "misled," and there were no beggars in London.

In his first article above referred to he told of his visit to the homes of the poorer classes in London those whose earnings were four to five dollars per week, and "how happily they lived," that their life was a free and easy one, they had no cares, etc. He further said that the London beggar was a myth, or that there were no more beggars in London than there were in New York or any other large American city.

In contradiction to the above, let me first say that London is a pest house of beggars. They can be found on every street corner and on every street; they are the poorest kind of beggars, and in many cases the dirtiest kind of beggars. They belong to that class that are not allowed to roam the streets of our American cities but are locked up for safe keeping.

Then, again, the comparison of the "happy life" of the poor working class would, were it not a solemn matter, be considered humorous. This class of people live in one or two rooms in the very poorest quarters of the city. and there are more poorer quarters in London to the thousand inhabitants than there are in New York to every five thousand ; they eat but little, and usually drink all the poor beer and whiskey they can get. Indeed they are a deplorable class.

Mr. Ralph's second letter was of the really humorous type, and even more ridiculous than his first. It was on the subject of "English vs. American Food." Said Mr. Ralph, "I was glad to go to London once more, and enjoy the good wholesome eating that her people are accustomed to ; it was such a relief from what we are accustomed to in America."

What could Ralph's past way of living have been if this utterance of his was true—but it was not true, and Ralph knew it, or else he was the worse specimen of an epicurean this country ever turned out. In England there is not the variety we have, the same meats and vege-

The Nightingale Tomb in Westminster Abbey, London.

tables, the same entrees and desserts are served up from January to January ; two vegetables, potatoes and one other, make up this course for every lunch or dinner. Their meats, with the exception of mutton, are never cooked correctly, while a good beefsteak is unknown. In the matter of dessert they are still subjects for a kindergarten. During our four months' tour of Europe, we stopped at the best hotels but they were no comparison to our best American hotels. On the continent they serve one better than in England, for they seasoned their food, while in England they do not.

A word on the subject of living. First, to live the same in Europe as we do here would cost from 20 to 30 per cent more in any country I visited. Second, they do not live the same over there as we do here. That really covers the whole matter in a nutshell. The average Britisher would live something like this :

For breakfast—rolls, eggs and coffee.

For lunch—beef, potatoes, peas, cheese and crackers.

For dinner—soup, beef, potatoes, cabbage, and either a pudding or fruit and coffee.

The above bill of fare is such as is usually served in a family who may be called " well to do." but not wealthy. Compare this with what a man with an income of $1500 per year would have in this country. When we consider the laboring classes, they live poor. Their breakfast is usually bread and coffee. At 10 o'clock they have a ten or fifteen minutes' recess for bread and tea ; at noon, a soup, bread and coffee, or a piece of beef, bread and coffee ; at 4 o'clock, another recess for bread and tea, and at night their supper consists of about the same. Meat only once a day—some have it at noon and some at night.

On the continent the working people live largely on bread and beer or cheap wine, with a soup or a bit of meat once a day, while the better class live better than does the average Britisher of the same rank.

The purchasing power of a dollar is greater in the United States than in Europe. This may seem strange to the average reader who has never been abroad, yet it is nevertheless true. Said a French lady to me about two months before I departed for the other side : " I was born in Paris, I know just how far a dollar will go there ; I can get more for one hundred dollars in Boston or New York than I can in any city I ever visited in Europe." She referred to the average purchase, and did not mean all kid gloves, all hose or any one thing, for each place you visit has its specialties. Gloves are cheaper in Paris or London than in New York, laces are cheaper in Brussels, works of art cheaper in Germany and Italy, diamonds cheaper in Amsterdam or London. Men's clothes are cheaper in London, but while you get good cloth you get poor workmanship. Furs are 50 per cent cheaper in Geneva and 20 per cent cheaper in London than in New York. On the other hand, underwear, shirts, hosiery, collars, cuffs, neckwear, shoes, ladies' undergarments and a thousand other small things are much higher wherever you go than here at home. Take silks for dresses; one has an idea they can be bought on the other side for a song, but you have my word for it, that you not only find a better assortment in our large stores here, but the prices are actually lower, and this in the face of the fact that we import the greater amount of what we use and pay 60 per cent duty on them. If you go to a really first-class dressmaker or a milliner, you will pay fully as much, if not more, for their services as you will for the same class of work here. I could name a hundred little things that cost from 25 to 100 per cent more on the other side than the self same article would cost here. Take the necessities of life, such as meats, poultry, eggs, butter, cheese, vegetables, etc., and they are higher at all seasons of the year than they are in the United States. And in the face of the above, the average pay of the working class is from 75 cents to $1 per day. No wonder they have to live economically.

While in London I attended an entertainment where a display of animated photographs illustrating the Queen's Jubilee procession was one of the attractions. These photographs were shown without interruption for twenty minutes and you can imagine my surprise when they commenced, the orchestra struck up the "Washington Post March," and it was continued during the show. This is an English theater. The next thing I looked for and expected to see was an English ballet, illustrating the Queen's Jubilee, danced to the tune of "Yankee Doodle."

The Captain got mixed up with his English money occasionally. One day he bought three cigars. I asked him how much he paid for them.

"Well," he remarked, "I think it was forty odd cents. I gave the clerk a shilling, thrippence, a penny and something else."

London was full of American flags. They floated from nearly every store. Walking up Regent street from Piccadilly to Oxford Circus, I counted no less than nine in one day, not little tiny flags, but full-sized American flags floating from flagstaffs on top of the buildings. Many of the stores were decorated with the American and English colors. Of course this was to attract business, but at the same time it showed there was a good feeling.

The question has been often discussed as to what is the cost for a tour of Europe. That certainly depends upon how the tourist in question desires to go. It can be made very expensive or inexpensive. To illustrate, I will take for instance a case where dollars and cents do not count and give an example of about the cost of a tour of three months:

Fare, round trip,	$200
Steamer fees,	15
Fare from Liverpool to London, second class,	10
Fare for continental tour, two months,	75
Fare two weeks' tour of England and Scotland,	25
Hotel two weeks in London,	56
Hotel two weeks England,	42
Hotel sixty days continent,	210
Tips,	35
Carriages,	25
Fees to galleries, museums, etc.	15
Laundry,	15
Total,	$723

or in other words about $800. In regard to the expense of the above let me say that the passage across and back includes that on one of the ocean greyhounds, like the Majestic or Teutonic. This price will pay for a berth in a two-berth inside room, or in a four-berth outside room on the lower deck. The accommodations, however, are strictly first-class. Higher rates of fare are charged for choice locations in outside rooms, and where rooms are taken as a whole, usually double fare is exacted. The steamer fees include 10s ($2.50) each for your room steward and table steward and 5s (1.25) for your deck steward, who looks after your steamer chair and your comfort while on deck.

It will be observed that I have put down the fare from Liverpool to London at second class, which is the usual way of traveling. The

The Marble Arch, Hyde Park, London.

two weeks' tour of England is also to be made second class, while the fare for the two months' tour of the continent is first-class steamers and second-class rail, excepting in France, where the conveyance is by first-class rail. It will also be observed that the rate for two weeks in London, or fourteen days, the hotel charge is about $4 per day. This is as low a figure as one can get in a first-class hotel. Most of the hotels are conducted on the European plan and a very few, for instance, "The Langham," which is one of the best hotels in London, will take guests on the American plan, at a nominal rate of $3.75 per day. As the Langham hotel is located in the very best part of London, on high land, with magnificent surroundings, there is no better house for one to stop, in case they want a first-class place—one of refinement and quiet. The average cost for hotels through England would be about $3.50 per day. These are also conducted on the European plan. On the continent the rate is about the same, provided best hotels are visited. There are many cheap hotels where lower rates can be had, but the average tariff is about as follows: Rooms $1 per day, plain breakfast, consisting of eggs, rolls, toast and butter and coffee, tea or chocolate, 50 cents. Table d'hote lunch, 75 cents. Dinner from $1 to $1.25. These are the prevailing prices in all the first-class hotels.

The estimate of $35 for tips will be sufficient, where one is traveling alone, as the amounts are usually very small, but a large number have to be looked after. It will also be observed in making an allowance of $25 for carriages, that this will be sufficient as one can usually hire a carriage for twenty-five cents in England; the rate, however, in France is thirty cents to which must be added the *pour boire*, or "drink money," of five cents extra. In most all the galleries, museums and places of interest, a small fee, varying from ten cents to twenty-five cents, is charged, which the $15 allowed for above will be ample to cover. The matter of laundry will be rather a surprise to the American tourist, as the Europeans have not yet adopted the American methods in this work. Usually it is horribly done and the prevailing prices are nearly as much as in this country. In case a party of two are traveling together, the total expenses will be somewhat less for each one than the above, for the reason that two can ride in a carriage at the same price as one; in other words, a carriage ride of twenty-five cents will convey two people without an additional charge, while in the matter of tips they will be increased but very little.

In addition to the above there are other expenses that will confront the tourist and they are preparations for the journey. For instance, a good steamer trunk will cost from $8 to $15, a steamer chair costs $1 each way, and there are other little incidentals that will be **necessary to make** the voyage a pleasant **one.**

Now comes the question of making an economical tour. This can be accomplished, as follows: There are many freight steamers, plying between **Boston,** New York and Liverpool, which convey passengers for the nominal fare of about $40 each way. The steamer fees are **less,** third-class railroad passage can be taken and the tourist can stop at **cheaper hotels, and** instead of carriages take omnibuses and **tram cars, thus** reducing the expenses considerably. Therefore, we might **figure it** up something **like this** :

Fares for round **trip,**	$ 80
Steamer fees,	8
Fare, third-class, to London and **return,**	7
Fare, third-class, continental **tour,**	55
Fare, two weeks' English tour,	18
Hotel, two weeks in London at $2 per day,	28
Hotel, two weeks in England at $2 per day,	28
Hotel sixty days on the continent at $2 per day,	120
Tips,	20
Fees to galleries, **museums,** etc.	15
Laundry,	15
Total,	$394

or one-half the **first estimate.**

In **many cases the tourist prefers to go to pensions** or boarding **houses, where accommodations can be had** in England as low as from **$1.25 to $1.50** per day, and on **the** continent from $1 to $1.25 per day. In **a** case like this it would be necessary **to** make a stop of several days to secure these rates. In lining out the continental tour it would include something like the following : Liverpool to London ; from London northward, visiting **the** English lakes ; thence to Glasgow, over The Trossachs to Edinburgh ; Edinburgh down through York and several other interesting **places to Harwich ; then by steamer to** Rotterdam, visiting Rotterdam, **the Hague, Amsterdam ; on** to Antwerp, Belgium ; Brussels ; thence to Cologne, Germany ; up **the Rhine to** Bierbich ; Frankfurt. Heidelberg, Nuremberg, Munich and a general tour of Switzerland, ending at Geneva; thence to Paris, with the privilege of a stop over at the Dijon ; Paris to London, where two weeks will be allowed to visit the city ; thence to Cambridge, Hampton Court, Windsor, Oxford, Warwick, Stratford-on-Avon, Chester and Liverpool.

Of course the above trip can be varied. The tourist can disembark at Queenstown and go through Ireland, crossing from Belfast to Glasgow and do Scotland, and then come down to London, if he prefers, before going on the continent, or else go directly on the continent.

The continental trip can be taken by going directly from Frankfurt to Leipsic, Berlin, and thence southward to Vienna, and then into Italy on the way to Switzerland. In this instance, of course, Heidelberg, Nuremberg and Munich would be omitted from the trip.

We were riding through a beautiful country park, when our attention was called to some blackbirds.

"What kinds of birds are those?" asked the Captain.

"English sparrows," was the reply from one of our party.

"Is that so?" remarked the first speaker. "Why, in our country we never saw a black English sparrow, and never a quarter as large as these."

The barber shops of Great Britain, and I might as well include the continent, are a curiosity. The chairs are little, low, stiff-backed seats, in which the customer squats himself and has his head jerked back with his face directed to the ceiling. The barber applies a little lather, runs over your face with a razor and then hands you a towel with which you go to the wash basin, clean your face, comb your hair and depart. The cost for such a luxurious shave as this is all the way from four to six cents, yet, as my friend, the Captain, said, "it was dear at any price."

What would an American tourist think if he were obliged to carry his bathtub with him? Yet, standing in the smoking room of my hotel, while in London, I saw a carriage drive up in front of an elegant mansion, where some of the family were about to go on a journey, for their baggage was brought out and with it a portable bathtub. It is not an uncommon thing for families to carry this necessary article with them while touring in Europe.

An interesting incident came to my observation while I was in Low's Exchange, Northumberland avenue, London. It was shortly

The Thames Embankment, London.

after the passage of the Dingley bill that I met two ladies here, evidently mother and daughter. They were from Cincinnati, for they were reading Cincinnati papers. The mother finally stopped short in perusing her paper and addressing her daughter said :

"Maria, look here, 'The buggy business is picking up, and everything indicates a prosperous season.' That is good news for us."

Maria glanced at her mother, and in return said :

"Maw, I am going to have that diamond ring, sure."

And from the look on maw's face, I am sure that Maria got her ring.

While in London I visited an art store and was much interested in a gentleman and lady who came in while I was there. I spotted them at once as fellow countrymen of mine. They wanted to buy some pictures. They looked over quite a number and the dealer was explaining to them the merits of a number of landscapes about 18x24 inches in size that were indeed very handsome pictures and were painted by well-known artists. They, however, did not please the lady. She insisted that what she wanted was a "big painting." She did not care who the artist was, as long as it was a good-looking picture and was "large in size." I did not ask them where they came from, but I am under the impression that they were Chicagoans.

I met a friend of mine in London who had a curiosity to show me. It was nothing more nor less than a string of beads that he had bought at the Vatican at Rome and which he treasured very highly. It seems that he paid $2 for the beads and that the owner of the stand or booth where he bought them, informed him that if he was willing to pay $3 more and would wait a few minutes, he would take them in and have the Pope bless them. My friend was only too glad to pay the extra amount, and the result was that in about ten minutes the dealer returned with the beads and the $3 extra was paid, and the best part of the story was that he believed the Pope had blessed them. I suggested that a sign might be placed up on the Vatican, something after this style, "Beads Blessed for $3 from 9 to 10 A. M. and from 3 to 4 P. M. This for the Benefit of Americans Only."

After doing London thoroughly, we prepared to make our way for the Continent. On the day before our departure, the Captain asked me in which direction we were bound.

"To Holland," I replied.

"Where?" asked the Captain.

"To Holland."

"Holland, Holland," remarked the Captain. "Now, old man, remember one thing, do not ask me to take a glass of gin. That is something I never touch," and the Captain felt happy in the thought that he had given me a temperance lecture, as we were about to enter Holland.

CHAPTER IV.

Doing Quaint Old Holland.

THE Captain is a great lover of art and decided to invest in a few pictures. In making his selection there was one by Fradille, an Italian artist, which very much pleased the Captain.

When I met him at the hotel on the evening of the purchase, he came up to me and remarked :

"I tell you I have got one of the finest pictures in the country, and, moreover, it is by that celebrated artist, Fra Diavolo."

> " What land is this that seems to be
> A mingling of the land and sea ?
> This land of sluices, dykes and dunes ?
> This water-net that tessellates
> The landscape ? This winding maze
> Of gardens, through whose latticed gates
> The imprisoned pinks and tulips gaze ;
> There in long summer afternoons
> The sunshine, softened by the haze,
> Comes streaming down as through a screen ;
> Where over fields and pastures green
> The painted ships float high in air,
> And over all and everywhere
> The sails of windmills sink and soar
> Like wings of sea-gulls on the shore ?"

So sang the poet.

The old saying that "God made the world, but the Dutch made Holland" was well put. The American tourist who visits the continent and misses Holland, is like seeing the play of Hamlet with Hamlet left out. Here is one of the most interesting countries on the other side of the water. Leaving London via Harwich (pronounced Harrich) at 8:30 P. M., the Parkestine Quay, where the boat leaves for the Hook of Holland, is reached at 9:58, and immediately the steamer departs and at 8:30 the next morning you are at Rotterdam, a city of 235,000 population and located on the right bank of the Maas. Rotterdam is the second largest city and the chief port of Holland, and has wonderful advantages as a harbor. The streets, a novel and

Typical Scene in Holland.

picturesque combination of water, bridges and trees, delight the visitor. Many of the canals are so deep that ocean vessels go through them in safety.

On arrival here we took a carriage and enjoyed a two hours' ride over the city. Among the interesting places visited was the Groote Market, where the peasantry were to be seen at their best, dressed in their quaint Dutch costumes and wooden shoes. The market wagons were such as our street hucksters use, and were propelled by dogs which were hitched up under the vehicle. Fruit and vegetables were here in abundance, fresh, clean and cheap. A basket, holding at least eight quarts, of the most delicious strawberries, and some of them as large as a half dollar, could be bought for twenty-five cents. Here in this market place once stood an old corner house, known as "The House of the Thousand Terrors." In 1572 when by stratagem the Spanish entered the town and massacred its people, a thousand of them sought refuge here, put up the shutters and barred the entrance, and killing a kid, let the blood run out under the doorway. The Spaniards seeing the red stream, concluded that the inmates had been dispatched, and passed on.

There is a good picture gallery here, but the subjects are not near so fine as at The Hague or Amsterdam. From Rotterdam we took the cars, and one hour's ride brought us to The Hague, positively the most beautiful spot in Holland. The Hague has a population of 180,000, and near here is the permanent residence of the child-queen, Wilhelmina. The city is lined with broad, clean streets, many canals and most beautiful and artistic residences. While Amsterdam is the commercial capital of Holland, The Hague is the seat of the government. Here is the residence of the Dutch court, the headquarters of Parliament and the abode of foreign ministers. From The Hague in 1660 sailed Charles II. on his restoration to the British throne, and twenty-two years later William III. of Orange left the city for England to take up the English crown and become William III. of Great Britain.

The Binnenhof, an irregular brick building, was once a castle of the courts of Holland. Within the courts of this place is the Hall of the Knights. Opposite this hall, one beautiful morning in May, 1619, Johannes Van Oldenbarneveld, prime minister of Holland, was put to death by command of Prince Maurice of Nassau, who was then stadt-

The Little Palace in the Woods, The Hague.

holder. The story is told how for years the prince and Johannes lived on terms of friendship and worked together for the good of their country, but bitter theological differences poisoned Prince Maurice against his old friend, and led to the latter's death.

At the northeast of the Binnenhof is the famous gallery of art, once the residence of the prince. Among the notable subjects here is Paul Potter's "The Bull," which was removed by Napoleon to Paris, when he invaded this city in 1795. Later it was returned. Some of Rembrandt's masterpieces are displayed here, "The Lesson, in Anatomy" being one of them.

While at The Hague, the Captain went into a barber shop to get shaved. After the operation was completed the barber asked him if he would have some corrispitsa on his face. The Captain looked at him for a moment and replied :

"No, sir, I never use kerosene on my face."

It will repay a visitor to Holland to take in the stores and notice the methods of doing business in this quaint country. Some of the wares are cheap. This is the home for delft, and it can be purchased here for about one-half the price in the United States. To the smoker this is the paradise for a good and yet a cheap cigar, as there is no duty on tobacco in Holland. I went into one of the cigar stores and asked for a twenty-five cent cigar (ten cents in our money), I thought the attendant had a case of heart disease. Ten cents (four in our money) is considered a high price to pay for a cigar while a really good smoke can be had for five cents, two American coppers.

Probably the most interesting place to visit at The Hague is the "Little Palace in the Woods" so styled. This gem of a spot is about a mile and a half from the center of the city. It is a royal villa, and was built by the widow of Prince Frederic of Orange. The drive from the main road is through an avenue shaded by tall trees, and is almost like fairyland. The walls and ceilings of the main hall, or dance room, are covered with paintings made to fit the spaces. This work is all of the Rubens school, and is something remarkable. The property belongs to the crown.

Three miles from The Hague is Scheveningen, the leading watering place of Holland. It is easily reached by a fine line of steam tram cars, and the ride is a delightful one. The scene on the beach is certainly an animated one, and the general surroundings are the same as

On the Beach at Scheveningen, Holland.

any of our popular watering resorts. The day we were there occurred the "procession of the flowers," taken part in by vehicles of all sorts gaily dressed with a profusion of beautiful flowers, ribbons, etc.

From The Hague we went to Amsterdam, the commercial capital of Holland, with a population of 450,000, and the largest city in the kingdom. Tourists say that Amsterdam rivals Venice for its canals. The city is bui t on piles, and covers no less than ninety islands, connected by over three hundred bridges. It is located on the river Wije (pronounced Wy). The most important thing to consider is, that the waters of the canals have to be kept on the move, so they will not become impure, while it is even more important that they have to be kept in check, to prevent the city from becoming inundated. This is all done by a system of sluices and dykes.

At Amsterdam the Captain's attention was attracted to a sign over a door that read "Tehuur." "There," said he, "that is your name in Dutch." When he had the word translated, he found it meant "To Let."

The royal palace is located on the west side of the Dam (the Dam is the main square of the city, and is located in the heart of the same). This building has no front entrance, but, as the Irishman said, "the front door is behind." The palace was presented to King Louis Napoleon in 1808, when he made this city his home. The principal sight in a tour of the inside is the main hall or dance room, which is 60x120 feet, and 100 feet high, without a single column of support. It is said to be the largest room of its kind in Europe.

The leading art gallery is the Rijks Museum (pronounced Ryks). It has a fine collection of paintings mostly of the Dutch school. "The Night Watch," by Rembrandt, and "Filial Love," said to be next to Rubens' masterpiece, are to be seen here. In addition to the gallery there is connected with the Rijks a fine museum of historic relics.

The diamond cutting industry is the chief business of the city, and employs about 50,000 hands, of which 10,000 are Jews. The Jewish population of the city is about 40,000, and they have their own special quarter where they live.

While I am writing about Holland it might be well to say a word about its girl queen, Wilhelmina, who on her eighteenth birthday, August 31, 1898, will be crowned Queen of Holland. Wilhelmina is

Rokin Canal, Amsterdam.

the last of the House of Orange, a house made famous three hundred years ago, through the bold military achievements of its greatest member, Wi liam the Silent. King William III., the father of the queen, spent the greater part of his life in wild dissipation. In 1839 he married Princess Sophia of Saxony. At this time he was Prince of Orange, but after ten years had passed he became king, and the fortune he received is said to have nearly turned his head, and he plunged into all sorts of dissipation, and finally alienated himself from his queen, whom he falsely accused of plotting with Emperor Napoleon to depose him and make her queen regent. Shortly after she died and left two sons. The oldest, the Prince of Orange, ruined his health and died, after a reckless life in Paris, while the other son, who was of unsound mind, soon followed his brother to the grave. Left without an heir, the king, who was fast aging, began to look around for a wife, and finally decided on the Duchess of Albany, who refused him. It is said that when this refusal was made known, her sister Emma made this remark to her: "Helen, I would never refuse to become a queen." The king, overhearing this remark, was pleased with the same, and addressed his offer of marriage to her, and true to her word she accepted him and became Queen Emma. The king was sixty-eight years and his wife nineteen years old. She bore him one child, Wilhelmina, and nursed him carefully until his death in 1890. A few years before his death, at a council of the States General, he obtained the setting aside of the old Salic law, which forbade a female heir to succeed to the throne, and upon his death Wilhelmina became queen, and her mother was appointed queen regent until she attained her majority. Under the faithful care of her mother Wilhelmina has developed into a healthy, lovable girl, and won the hearts of her Dutch subjects.

While visiting the Rijhs Gallery at Amsterdam, the attendant was describing at some length Rembrandt's remarkable picture of "The Night Watch." The Captain looked on, but his patriotism got the best of him, for he whispered to me, "It may have been a big fight but it didn't stand a show beside the Battle of Bull Run."

July 4, 1897, saw a party of thirty American citizens and "citizenesses" at the Hotel Amstel, Amsterdam, Holland. As our National fete day came on Sunday we determined to celebrate it on Monday. The stars and stripes floated all day the 4th and 5th from the top of

Achterburgwal—Old Part of Amsterdam.

the hotel and we would occasionally go outside to catch a glimpse of "Old Glory." Monday morning a breakfast was prepared in the main dining hall, and we marched in at promptly 9 o'clock. There a surprise awaited us. The hall was beautifully decorated with our flags and the table was covered with not only little emblems of our pride but beautiful flowers, and then sat down thirty live Yankees as full of patriotism as if we had been at home. After the repast, it became my lot to take the head of the table, and conduct the feast to come. Addresses were made by my friend the Captain, and others, but the Captain gave us a regular Fourth-of-July oration.

So much from our visit to Deutschland.

At our hotel in Amsterdam the Captain got in conversation with an Englishman. During the talk the Captain mentioned Boston, and his companion asked him " if Boston was in New York." I could see my companion was lying in wait for sweet revenge. It came sooner than I expected, for the Englishman asked the Captain something about London. "London, London," answered the Captain, "where is London?"

And I had nearly three months to look ahead, and the Captain was to be with me all that time.

CHAPTER V.

Antwerp, Brussels and Cologne.

I HAVE had more trouble with the Captain. He insists I am no kind of a man to go around with, "as I walk too much," yet sometimes I feel like flying. While at the Antwerp gallery we were shown De Vriendt's celebrated painting of "The Judgment of Solomon," Our guide was telling us about this wonderful work of art, and I found myself lost in rapture, but quickly recovered myself, when the Captain gave me a punch and asked : " Do you suppose this picture refers to my friend Salomon, the leather manufacturer ? "

Before I give the story of my stay in Antwerp, Brussels and Cologne, it may be interesting to know this chapter is written in my room at the Hotel Disch, Cologne, with the great spires of the cathedral before my eyes. It is a beautiful July afternoon. Tired with the sights of the city, I have repaired to my hotel, thrown open the sashes of my window, and seated myself at a desk directly in front of it, and within possibly 500 feet of this great historic church. The summer sun casts its brilliant rays over one of the most magnificent piles in all Europe.

Leaving Amsterdam, after a ride of four hours, we arrived at Antwerp, the second largest city in Belgium, with a population of 250,000. Antwerp has special facilities as a commercial center, and by a splendid system of docks made by Napoleon I., can accommodate 2000 ships. The arms of the city are two hands, representing *ant*, a hand, *werpen*, to throw, which were derived from a certain giant, Antigonus, who cut off the hands of those who would not pay toll, and threw them into the river. This is said to have been continued by him until he was conquered by another giant, Brabo.

The churches here are embellished with some of the best productions of Rubens, Van Dyck, and others. In the Notre Dame can be seen "The Descent from the Cross," Rubens' masterpiece. The original is a small picture, and is to be seen in the gallery. It was

Milk Venders, Antwerp.

after the completion of this that Rubens painted the large one. Here is also "The Elevation of the Cross," also by Rubens, and the "Assumption of the Virgin," by the same artist, possibly 15x25 feet, with thirty-two life-size faces. This great work was completed in just sixteen days. The center of the dome was nine months in completing, and was done by an artist who lay on his back. This dome is 133 meters high, and is reached by a staircase of 622 steps. The chimes are among the most curious in Europe, and consist of 99 bells, on which any selection can be played, or, as it was explained to me by my guide, "It plays every known tune, either sacred or profane." Rubens died here in 1640, and was buried in St. Jacques Church. The Antwerp art gallery contains many notable pictures by celebrated artists, and many representations of the Flemish school.

In our party were two charming ladies from the West. They shopped and shopped galore. While at Antwerp they purchased $175 worth of lace. Some of the party gave them a short lecture on their extravagance.

"Why," was the reply, "we are all right. The cost of this trip was defrayed by our father as a present, and our husbands gave us each $500 to spend."

"Such being the case," replied the first party, "you ought to take them both a present."

"We are going to do so, and have selected what we propose to take, and expect to buy them this afternoon," was the answer.

That evening, in the court yard of the hotel, the ladies were displaying the presents bought for husband and father. "Here is a meerschaum pipe for my husband. Isn't it lovely?" exclaimed one. "And to think, it only cost $1.20. I saw a beauty for $2.50, but I did not feel like paying so much. Then we bought this elegant piece of bronze for papa, the dear old soul; he paid all our expenses on this trip."

"What did we pay for that, Ella?" asked the other.

"Three dollars," was the reply. "And have you got Charley's present?"

"Yes; I bought him this lovely necktie for two francs (forty cents). I know he will be pleased with it."

The Captain nudged me and remarked that there was a case where the "loved ones at home" were not forgotten.

Palace of the Count of Flanders, Brussels.

The Plantin Museum is located here, and is the only one of its kind in existence. Christopher Plantin was the first great printer known, and was the publisher of the early different translations of the Bible in all the different languages. He also published all religious works of the King of Spain, Philip II. The house has been preserved in exactly the state in which it was left over 300 years ago, with its different workshops, etc., and here are shown the original manuscripts, publications, presses, type, wood cuts and proofs copperplates and proofs, in their original state.

Antwerp is adorned with a system of fine boulevards and squares, that make an interesting sight in a two hours' drive over the city.

Less than one hour's ride from Antwerp, we reach Brussels, the capital of Belgium, the largest city in the kingdom, with a population of 500,000, well called "The Little Paris," and by many tourists said to be the gayest city in Europe next to the French capital. A visit to the Hotel de Ville will repay one. This magnificent building was erected in the fifteenth century. It is gothic in its architectural style, and is 200x165 feet, with a spire 364 feet high. The architect hanged himself in the door of the spire after the building was completed on account of not getting the spire in the center of the building. The Hotel de Ville is the town or city hall of Brussels. The aldermanic chamber is small but magnificent in all its appointments. The walls are hung in tapestries three hundred years old, while the ceiling was painted by one of the old masters. Leading out of this are ante-rooms all finely and elaborately furnished with old tapestried walls. The next room that attracts attention is "the marriage hall.' Here all who marry in Brussels, must come. The mayor ties the knot. There are two entrances one for the rich for which "all who enter" must pay one hundred francs ($20) which fee goes to the poor and another entrance for the poor. There is no fee for the ceremony.

The Captain had got tired of having this and that picture by Rubens explained and described. When we got to Brussels and drove up in front of the Wirtz gallery, the Captain asked me, "What place is this?" I told him, and as we alighted, he asked. "Is there any of old Robbins' pictures in here? If so, I want to skip them."

The Wirtz gallery contains some of the most remarkable paintings in Europe, largely of an allegorical nature, many hideous in design yet interesting to the lover of art. The residence of King Leopold II.

King's Palace, Brussels.

is a fine old palace, pleasantly situated at the head of a parkway, and a main thoroughfare runs through the center of the park to the Houses of Parliament which face the palace. Adjoining the residence of the king is that of his brother, the Count of Flanders.

He who visits Brussels and does not go out to the battlefield of Waterloo, misses one of the greatest historic sights in Europe. We of the nineteenth century can hardly believe that so famous a fight was fought in such a small compass, a space of probably not over half a mile square. It was not a battle of guns and cannons, but a hand to hand fight. This spot may be reached in two different ways. The first by carriage ride, passing the old church where are erected twenty-eight tombs in memory of English, German and Hanoverian officers who fell at the battle. The second route is by rail direct.

Arr ving at Waterloo, the first thing that attracts one's attention is a mound in the center erected to secure a better view of the place. This is ascended by 225 steps; on the extreme top in the center is a large monument of a lion. From here is obtained a fine view of the whole field. Directly in front of you, after you reach the summit, you will find between the Chaussee de Nivelles and the Chaussee de Charleroi the Hollow of Ohain, so called. This is the spot where so many French cuirassiers fell in the early stages of the battle. Right and left are the obelisques erected to the memory of the Hanoverian officers and the column recalling the death of Lieut.-Col. Alex. Gordon, aide de camp to Wellington, who had taken up his position about here. A little beyond, in the direction of the village of Waterloo, is the farm of Mont St. Jean, which was turned into a hospital during the battle. Close by lies buried the leg of Lord Uxbridge, which he lost in the fight, and ordered buried here himself. On the other side, to the right, near the Chaussee de Nivelles is the Hougomont farm where the first shots of the battle were exchanged, and where traces of the bloody encounter are still discernible. This is the point where the French, leaning on the old guard, began to develop themselves, confronting in the distance, to the left, Wellington's lines. Immediately to the right stands the farm of Belle Alliance, the place where Wellington and Blucher met after their victory. To the left of this farm is the monument erected to the Prussian officers who fell, and beyond this is the village of Plancenoit, where Napoleon stood.

In our civil war there were many battles fought that for numbers of soldiers and intense fighting far surpassed that of Waterloo, but

Field of Waterloo, Near Brussels.

tor fierceness, probably nothing of its kind has occurred since that memorable contest.

They say it is the custom at continental hotels, where the tourist does not tip liberally to place the hotel labels on the baggage down in the corner and upside down. The Captain heard of this and it was with pride that he exhibited his trunks and bags to his fellow passengers and told them that every label was on uniformly, with the right side up.

"There is not a mean hair in my head," said the Captain.

And if the Captain ever spoke the truth, it was on this occasion.

Cologne has a population of over 300,000, yet one would think it scarcely so large by a tour of the city. I suppose this is the most Catholic city in Germany. In former years it was the seat of these people, being one of the oldest cities in central Europe, dating back before the Frankish kings of 460. In 1350 the Jews were expelled from here, and the city was walled in.

It is indeed interesting to walk around the business portion and view the stores, most of which are modern and up to date, yet there are portions of the city that still show signs of its antiquity. Of course the most interesting object here is the Dom or cathedral, said to be one of the finest in the world. St. Peter's at Rome and St. Paul's at London are both magnificent specimens of architecture, the former the largest, and the latter the third largest in size in the world, the second being the cathedral at Milan; but something in the grandeur of the Dom surpasses all these. Commenced on Aug. 14, 1248, the building was just 632 years in process of completion, as it was not finished until Aug. 14, 1880. It is 496 feet long and 238 feet wide through the transept. It is built in the shape of a cross, and is 200 feet high. The stained glass windows are its chief ornamentation, as there are no oil paintings of note here. The many windows and the artistic design of the glass arch are worth going many a mile to see.

Looking out upon this magnificent structure, which looms up before me as I write, I am reminded of the legend of its architecture, so different from that of other cathedrals. It is a story well worth repeating.

The great Dom or cathedral was built, so tradition says, about the middle of the thirteenth century, by Conrad of Hochsteden, then

Cathedral at Cologne.

Archbishop of Cologne, who resolved to erect the largest and most magnificent temple in the world ; so he began to look around for an architect, and finally secured one right at home. This architect was commissioned to draw plans and given one year in which to complete them. He labored for ten months, and at the expiration of that time his work was as unsatisfactory to the Archbishop as it was to himself. Time passed and the year was nearly up. The architect was in despair. Three days before the time appointed to meet his employer, he wandered into the forests of Siebengebirge, disconsolate and almost heartbroken, for he had hoped to build a church that would not only have been a monument for the world to look at, but would honor himself as well. Night drew on and a fearful tempest raged ; no object could be seen, so fierce was the darkness, yet this did not disturb him half so much as the thoughts of the hour to come, when he expected to be covered with shame and mockery. Suddenly a flash of lightning struck an oak tree near by, and a fearful clap of thunder followed. The oak burned brightly, and the terrified architect saw a man step out of the flames. In appearance he looked like a poacher, yet he wore a red mantle and a broad brimmed hat with a feather.

"A terrible storm, Dom Architect," he said. "How could you wander here? Follow me, and I will conduct you out of the woods."

These remarks were like bitter mockery to the man. To be called Dom Architect, and he had done nothing. He turned in another direction. The new arrival, however, called to him, and producing a bottle requested him to drink. This was at first refused, but after a second request, he lifted the bottle to his mouth and drank. Like fire it ran through his veins. He drank the second time, and then, feeling so good, gave attention to his companion, who said :

"I see you have no confidence in me, yet I am the only one who can help you. My conditions are easy," and with that he drew a parchment from his pocket, unrolled it, and displayed to the astonished architect the plans of the great cathedral. The architect was for a moment dazzled. Here was the very plan he had dreamed of.

"I will cede this to you on one condition—a trifle—that you sign this bond with your own blood," and presenting a paper to the man awaited his reply, which was almost instantaneous. The bond was signed, the man disappeared, the storm ceased, and the architect went home and the next day astonished the archbishop with his documents. They were promptly accepted and the building commenced. As it progressed it was decided to place a plate in front with the name of the architect thereon.

Time passed, the man grew sad, and finally confessed all and asked for help to save his soul. The archbishop promised his help and sent him to a hermit in the Eifel mountains, who was said to have control over evil spirits. The hermit promised to aid him by continuous prayer, and after a season with him he was sent home, and told if he lived a pious, repentant life the balance of his days Satan would never have control over him. This the architect did, and the building of the cathedral progressed, although not under his direction. Some years later he died, and the same night the tablet that bore his name disappeared from the building.

Tradition says that by dispute, envy and hatred the Evil One succeeded in interrupting the building of the temple, yet work progressed from time to time, but it was only on the 14th of August, 1880, over 600 years after it was started, that the last scaffold was taken down, and the grand Dom pronounced completed.

The night before our departure from Cologne, the Captain and I were seated together in the courtyard of our hotel, enjoying a cigar, when turning to me, the Captain remarked:

"Where do we go from here?"

"Tomorrow," I replied, "we start on our trip up the Rhine."

"The Rhine," inquired the Captain, "it seems to me, I have heard of that before."

"Yes," was my reply, "it is said to be the most picturesque river in the world."

"River," answered the Captain, "why, I thought the Rhine referred to some kind of beer or wine."

And then I got up and as it was a beautiful moonlight night, I took a lonely walk around the block.

CHAPTER VI.

A Day on the River Rhine.

"I'VE heard so much talk about the Rhine river that I want to see it," remarked the Captain to me.

When I told him that we would go from Cologne to Biebrich or, in other words, we would go up the Rhine from this point, and it would be a half day's journey, from 8:45 A. M. to 8:45 P. M., the Captain was delighted. He had heard of steamers that would beat the Fall River Line, yet he had never seen them, and again he was doomed to disappointment, for the largest and best steamer that courses the Rhine is no better than our ordinary harbor boats. I think the Captain would have enjoyed the day had he not met an Englishman on the boat just as we were leaving Cologne, and that individual rather poked fun at the Captain, "because the President of the United States was an Irishman."

"What do you mean by that?" asked the Captain of him.

"Why, your President," was the reply.

"Well, what of our President?"

"Why, McKinley—he's an Hirishman. Could not you fellows find a Hamerican?"

The Captain puffed away on his fifteen pfennig cigar, and it was some moments before he could recover himself to reply, and inform his English companion that McKinley was not an Irishman.

Well, to our story. We left Cologne at 8:45 and started on our trip up the Rhine. The first place of interest to pass was Deutz, on the left; we then passed Westhofen, Ensen and numerous other picturesque towns until we arrived at Bonn, a beautiful place of 25,000 to 30,000 people, and the first stopping place of the "Express steamers." Bonn is properly celebrated as the birthplace of Beethoven, and the house in which he was born still stands at No. 20 Bonngasse. There is a legend connected with Bonn well worth repeating.

Toward the latter part of the seventeenth century, when the people of this town were recovering from the oppressions of war, there lived

Old Castle on the Rhine, Near Coblenz.

here a young locksmith. He hoped to be able to join his father at Endenich, but as the old man had lost all his property the son was unable to go there and run the risk of living on his bounty. In deep affliction the old man resolved that if his boy could not come to him he must content himself to pass the remainder of his life in company with his only other child, also a son. Konrad, the locksmith, kept at his work, and made a good living, and apparently prospered until he fell in love with the daughter of a sheriff, named Gretchen Heribet, whose father did not look with favor on the suit. Sheriff Heribet had apparently become impoverished by the war, but suddenly began to show signs of great prosperity. His burned houses were rebuilt, his mortgages paid off, and he showed riches that he formerly did not possess or could not honestly obtain by his own labor. This caused comment among the neighbors. Some believed his wealth came from supplying the enemy, others from finding hidden treasure, while some believed he was in connection with goblins to whom he had sold his soul.

With the increase of wealth the sheriff grew proud and haughty, and finally regarded his fellow citizens with contempt. In the meantime Konrad had won Gretchen's heart, and could only hope to gain her father's consent to their marriage by some strategy, but one day in a fit of rage the sheriff struck Konrad, and then vowed vengeance, not only on his daughter's lover, but on his aged father as well. Rich villain that he was, the sheriff knew how to carry out his plans, and ere long Konrad's father found himself pressed by his creditors and the sale of his property and his own ruin imminent.

One night, after Konrad had managed to meet his love and been discovered by her father who drove him off, he repaired to his room in sadness, where in a gloomy state he sat until midnight, when, arousing himself, he bethought to call the goblins to his aid. Three times he did so, and the terrible Lapp appeared before him.

"What do you wish of me?" he asked.

"I demand gold. Help me to it," was Konrad's reply.

Lapp beckoned him to follow, and conducted him to the depths of a forest, then, pointing to a spot, disappeared. Konrad hastened home, fell in a fever that lasted several days, and then again visited the spot, where, after digging for a long time, he found a chest filled with gold. Taking out a supply, he returned to Bonn, bought a house, and in the meanwhile, piece by piece, brought the balance of the treasure to his home, conducted his business on a larger scale, and his success was thought to be due to his genius.

One of the first things Konrad did was to pay his father's debts, release his mortgages, and make the old man happy. In short, Konrad eclipsed the sheriff by his mode of living and splendid surroundings, and it was an easy task to win his consent for Gretchen's hand, and in a short time the marriage took place.

After the marriage the young wife was not content until she found out how her husband had gained his wealth, and after teasing him for a long time he was about to tell her, when one night the officers of justice forced their way into his house, arrested him and put him in prison, and, after torturing him, he explained that he had found a treasure. This satisfied them for a while, and his wife was allowed to visit him, and in a brief hour of sweet interview he confessed all to her and was overheard. He was finally released, and told if he could prove his assertion he would be allowed to retain his wealth, but just as Konrad was on the point of doing this, the Jews in Bonn raised a great cry that one of their people, the rich Abraham, had suddenly disappeared during a journey and been murdered. Consequently, suspicion rested on the young locksmith, and he was again arrested.

Behind the prison walls Konrad was again tortured to make a confession, and in a foolish moment admitted that he was a party to the murder of the Jew, but that the deed was done by his father-in-law, who shot him, Konrad preferring to criminate him, as he had been the cause of all his troubles. The sheriff was arrested, and after torture confessed that he committed the deed. Both men were sentenced to be executed, and were dragged to the execution place, when an unexpected appearance demonstrated Konrad's innocence.

A Jew, just returned from a long wandering, happened to pass by and asked the cause of all the commotion, and when told, demanded that the proceedings stop, as he was Abraham. Both men were released. The impression on Konrad was severe. He and his wife left Bonn and removed to Endewich where his father lived and afterward died. The young couple lived for some time but were childless, and as they were wealthy devised that upon their death their all should go to charitable institutions and churches. Thus ended the story of Konrad and Gretchen.

The Captain was enjoying the scenery, as we were passing along the river, when one of the waiters on the boat brushed past him. As he came back, the Captain caught him by the arm and remarked :
"Sprechen sie Deutsch?"
"Yah," was the reply.
"Einschiffen Verbauften Gesselshaft," replied the Captain.
The waiter looked at him in amazement and the Captain was waiting for his reply. Finding it did not come, he looked at the man and said in English :
"Are you not a German?"
"Yes" answered the waiter in almost as good English as that of the Captain, "but I did not come from the same part of Germany that you did."
And as the waiter passed by, the Captain turned to me with a look as if he had been insulted.
"What do you think of that?" he remarked.
"Well," was my reply, "what were you trying to say to the man?"
"I asked him in good German what was the next place we stopped at?"
"Well, Captain," I replied, "you might have asked him in good German, but as near as I could get at it, you asked him something about 'embarking at an evaporation machine.'"
And as the Captain turned his back on me, he replied that my education in German had been sadly neglected.

From Bonn we sail on, and almost directly opposite lies the village of Beuel and farther on Kudinghoven, with a beautiful old castle formerly belonging to the Teutonic order. From the steamer may be seen the beautiful gardens and villas of the Coblenza-strasse. A little further on is Obercassel with an old church tower of the eleventh century and the viaduct by which the railway crosses the Rhine. And still further on lies Godesberg with the ruins of Godesberg castle on a basalt 86 meters high. This was built by Archbishop Dietrich and finished in 1349. In the war between the archbishop and the elector of Waldburg, who had become Protestant, it was in 1583 stormed by the Bavarians. From here to Niederdallendorf, about an hour's walk, is an ancient Cistercian abbey, built 1202–1233. This was destroyed and rebuilt in the sixteenth century, and during the French rule it was

sold and abolished. A lovely path leads along the side of the Petersberg to Konigswinter. At the left side of the road, to the Drachenfels, are the remains of an old castle bestowed by the Emperor, Henry II., upon the nunnery of Diet-kirchen, near Bonn.

The wines from this section are considered excellent, and are called Drachenblut (blood of the dragon) for here it is said was the spot where Siegfried killed the dragon, likewise the spot where Detrich of Bern s fight with Eck on the Menzenberg. From Drachenfels a path leads over the Wolkenberg, formerly a castle, to the Oelberg. A little further on we come to Lowenberg, with the ruins of an old castle. Here the elector, Count Wied, had secret meetings with Melancthon and Bucer in 1541, before he became a Protestant, and the Elector Gebhard of Waldburg fled from here when persecuted by the Bavarians on account of his marriage with Agnes of Mansfield, an escaped nun from the convent of Gerresheim.

From Konigswinter there is a road along the Rhine to the famous nightingale wood, where St. Bernard is said to have brought all the nightingales he had taken away from the gardens of the convent Hemerode, because they disturbed the nuns at prayer.

Opposite Konigswinter lies Mehlein. From here can be made an interesting trip over the extinct volanco Rodderberg to Rolandsbeck. There is now a farm in the crater of the volcano. In former years a gallows stood near here, and the story is told of a young man who was executed for murdering his sweetheart. After the execution she appeared, having been visiting her parents in a distant village, and it was then discovered that the accuser was a rival who had been rejected by the girl. The remains of an old castle stand here. This was built in the twelfth century by Archbishop Frederick I., and destroyed in the wars of Charles the Bold. Excursions can be made from here to Landskrone and the Ahrvalley with an old parish church in the Romanesque style, finished in 1246. Here is also an old cemetery with part of the walls in Roman. The portal with its relief belonged to a church of the ancient Christians. The different devices are represented by animals as in the Apocalypse, signifying that nothing unclean can enter the heavenly Jerusalem, but must remain outside the gates.

I had given the Captain the above account, and he appeared much interested, he listened attentively, and when I got through he turned to me and said :

"Where did you get that information?"

"It's a matter of history," I answered.

"History," replied the Captain. "I don't believe it. If the truth was known, I believe you are interested in some scheme to cut up this territory in house lots, and you are planning to work me in the deal."

Just then the orchestra struck up the overture from "William Tell," and I was for the moment saved from any further thought about jumping overboard.

The next stopping place we came to was Coblenz, a city of considerable size and of much importance. Here is located an old castle built in 1786, and has many attractions for one who wishes to give up a day to sight seeing. From Coblenz on to Biebrich is the most interesting part of the Rhine. Here commence the old castles and beautiful scenery. For five or six hours one has a feast before him. Just above Coblenz is Boppard. Here is a story told in connection with it:

Bayer of Boppard was a knight and scion of one of the noblest families of the Rhine country, young and rather wild, yet good natured. He loved Maria, a maiden of great beauty, who lived in a near-by castle. In due season they were engaged, and shortly after the knight went on a chase with some friends who were all bachelors. They teased him to that extent that upon his return he wrote his lady love, breaking the engagement. Not long after this the knight was out in the forest and met a stranger, who advanced and told him to prepare for a life or death struggle, as he was Maria's brother, and proposed to avenge her wrongs. The knight drew his sword, and a fierce combat followed, in which the stranger was wounded, and as he was helpless, the knight opened his helmet, and was astounded to behold the face of the beautiful Maria.

"Without you my life would have been unhappy," she murmured, "and by your hand I wished to die."

The knight strove to save her life, but in vain. She died, and he fell over her body senseless, where he was found by some of his friends and taken home and nursed to health. One of his first acts was to build a convent over her grave, and to call it Marienburg, after which he bequeathed all his property to it and then departed to Palestine, where he joined the Crusaders, hoping to find his death and rejoin his love; but for years he gained renown and victory, and at last, at the storming of the Fortress Ptolomais, being the first to ascend the ladder, he fell, a victim of the enemy.

The noon hour arrived, and our party entered the dining room of the steamer for our dinner. The Captain took his usual seat by my side.

"How is this dinner served?" he asked of the waiter.

"You can have it here table d'hote, or in the other saloon a la carte," was the reply.

"I go to the other saloon," remarked the Captain, as he got up to leave.

"Why so?" I asked.

"Because I want just what I want, and nothing more."

I asked him what he was hankering for, and he rather took me back by calling a waiter and ordering "An oyster stew and a piece of apple pie."

"Vont you hab sum leedle neck clams und sum showder?" asked the waiter. "Ve haf no Yankee dishes mit us."

The Captain took a table d'hote dinner.

Above Bomhofen is the ruined castle of the Two Brothers. Heinrich and Conrad were their father's pride, both brave, chivalrous and true sons. In the same castle lived an orphan girl, Hildegarde, who grew up in the family, who were relatives. The brothers knew her from childhood and loved her as a sister, until Conrad showed such affection that it was finally decided he was to marry her, but the ceremony could not take place until the completion of a new castle to be called Sternberg, near the Liebenstein castle in which his father lived. Heinrich could not bear to witness the ceremony and, while he loved his brother, he decided to leave home, go to Palestine and join the Crusaders and with him went many knightly youths and young men of the Rhine.

Shortly after Heinrich's departure his father was taken ill, and the day Castle Sternberg was completed he died. According to the customs of the country, the marriage had to be postponed one year. In the meantime Heinrich had so distinguished himself on the field of battle that his fame had become general, and Conrad determined to take a hand in the fight, and, bidding his bride good-by, departed. Not meeting with the same success his brother had, he started to return home and, while at Constantinople, met a beautiful Greek lady, and finally married her and took her to his home on the Rhine. When Hildegarde heard this her heart was broken, for with the return

of her faithless lover followed a season of festivities. Late one night a strange knight appeared at the Liebenstein Castle, and the next morning Hildegarde was shown to him, and surprised to find it was Heinrich, who had heard of his brother's wrong, and had returned to Hildegarde, and requested that she keep it a secret for a few days. On the fourth day after his arrival he sent a confidant to his brother, and challenged him to mortal combat. The challenge was accepted, and the fight was to take place the next day. The hour arrived, the swords were drawn, when Hildegarde appeared, forbade the struggle, and said she would repair to a convent. The brothers in the meanwhile made up their grievances, and it soon transpired that Conrad's wife was in secret correspondence with a young knight who lived near by, and shortly after she eloped with him. Both brothers took up their home in Castle Liebenstein, and Sternberg was deserted, and since their death the two old castles have stood there as a monument to them.

Above the Two Brothers are the ruins of the old Castle Maus, built in 1363. In the stream above St. Joan is a high hill with a sharp, rocky edge, a portion of which forms a profile of Napoleon. This is something after the Old Man of the Mountain, at the Profile House, Franconia Notch, N. H. Here the Rhine is the narrowest, and just above is a group of rocks called, "The Seven Maidens." According to the legend, they were the ladies of the Castle of Schonburg, who had hearts as cold as flint stones. The town of Wesel, with some attractions, comes next, and above that lies Schonburg, where Count Frederick Hermann was born. He served under various kings, and at the age of 72 fell at the Battle of the Boyne.

In the middle of the Rhine, upon a rocky island above Oberwesel, is the Pfalz, an old castle built in the fourteenth century by the Emperor Louis. In 1504 the castle was besieged by William of Hesse for six weeks, but without success. Napoleon had it destroyed in 1805. Many places of interest abound all along the river on both sides. We shortly come to Nollich and the Castle Nollinger, where a knight once rode up the jagged rocks called the devil's ladder, and won the hand of the fair daughter of the castle.

"Say, Captain," I remarked, as we were leaning back in our seats and viewing two old castles on the river bank. "Aren't those magnificent?"

"You may think so," was the only reply.
"Well, and don't you?" I asked.
"No," returned the Captain, "I don't."
"Why?" I replied.
"Well, I ll tell you why," said the Captain, as he straightened himself up and lit his cigar. "You told me I would see romantic old palaces, yet what do I behold but a lot of old ruins? I am wondering if you are trying to bunco me," and the Captain turned his back on me, and taking from his pocket a copy of the Bethel, Me., "Advertiser," he amused himself reading the town locals.

Lorch next attracts our attention. It is an old town and dates back over 1000 years. Near Lorch is the ruins of the former castle Furstenec. Here, it is said, lived Knight Oswald, owner of the castle, who was an excellent archer, and a bitter enemy of a neighboring nobleman, Wilm Von Saneck, who attempted to get Oswald in his power and finally succeeded, imprisoned him in a tower and deprived him of his sight. At first it was believed he had been killed by robbers, but his only son, Edwin, knowing of Von Saneck's malice, had suspicion he was the cause of his father's disappearance, so, disguising himself as an itinerant singer, when near the tower he rested, and a stranger passing got into conversation with him, and Edwin, by singing a sweet song, soon learned from him that a knight and his servant were imprisoned there. After the stranger departed, Edwin strolled up to the house, heard the sounds of jollity within, and entering sang a song, much to the amusement of all the party, who were under the influence of wine. Here he heard Von Saneck admit he had Oswald a prisoner and had deprived him of his eyesight. A wager was made by one that, even blinded as he was, Oswald could hit a given object with his arrow, and he was sent for by Von Saneck. Edwin saw his poor father brought in, a bow and arrow was given him and he was told to hit a cup on the table, but instead he shot Von Saneck through the heart and he fell dead. Edwin immediately sprang to the side of his father and said he would defend his act with his sword. The company made no protest and he departed with his sightless parent, conducted him home, and, although he could not restore his sight, made his last days peaceful and happy.

Upon the rock of the Soonwald are the ruins of Castle Sooneck, built in 1015, destroyed by Rudolph of Habsburg in 1282. The robber knights of Sooneck were executed here. Below was built, by the knights of Waldeck, the church of St Clements for the repose of the souls of the robber knights. A little beyond is Assmaunshausen, where the cream of German red wine is grown. Next is Bingerloch with Castle Ehrenfelds, built in 1210 by Philip of Rolanden, later the residence of the Archbishop of Mayence, destroyed by the French in 1689.

A soldier of the legion lay dying at Algiers.
There was lack of women's nursing, there was dearth of women's tears.
But a comrade stood beside him, while his life blood ebbed away,
And bent with pitying glance to hear each word he had to say.
The dying soldier faltered as he took that comrade's hand,
And he said, "I never more shall see my own, my native land.
Take a message and a token to some distant friends of mine,
For I was born at Bingen, fair Bingen on the Rhine."

What school boy or merchant of today but has heard, "Bingen on the Rhine?" It is a dear old town with about 7000 population. Here is a great wine market. An old parish church of the fifteenth century, with a Romanesque crypt of the eleventh century stands here. Above the town rises the Drususberg with Castle Klopp, destroyed by the French in 1689 and 1712. Just below is Rudeshein, famous for its wines. The robber knight lived here and was condemned to death by Archbishop of Mayence in 1282. The old castle, or what is left of it, still stands.

"I say," said the Captain to one of the deck hands, who could speak English, "what is that sign up there, which reads, '*Rauchen ist Verboten?*'"

"Smoking forbidden," was the reply.

"And that one over there?" asked the Captain.

"Talking with the pilot forbidden," was the answer.

"And there is another one," said the Captain.

"That means, spitting on the floor forbidden."

Just then the Captain's patience gave out, and turning to the waiter, he remarked:

"If I lived in a country like this I would commit suicide."

"Ah, Mein Herr, that is forbidden here," was the reply of the waiter, as he walked forward.

Here is a couple of short stories in connection with this country. The first is about Bingen, and goes to show how Hatto, Bishop of

Old Castle on the Rhine, Near Bingen.

Fulda, wished to obtain the vacant Archbishopric of Mayence. By means of bribery, trickery, etc., he succeeded, although there were many more worthy candidates. After his elevation, Hatto became proud and tyrannical. He taxed his people to erect large buildings to satisfy his love of splendor, tolls were imposed and new burdens forced upon them. Below Bingen he built a strong tower, opposite to which stands the ruins of Ehrenfels and the Castle Rhinestein, so that all passing ships could be stopped and tolls secured. Later on a terrible famine visited this country, and Hatto was in possession of all the product of the last harvest, and only allowed his stores sold at fabulous prices, consequently the general misery was increased. The people prayed for help, but he turned a deaf ear to them. At last, in their frenzy, the people forced themselves upon him and his friends while at a feast, and implored his aid; this he promised, and told them to go to a certain barn where grain was stored. After he had them secured therein, he ordered the doors fastened and the building set on fire, exclaiming, "With rebels, I treat them as I do mice, burn them." But, alas, just deserts awaited this cruel man, for with the burning of the barn, an army of mice came out and covered the place, and Hatto was obliged to flee to a ship, but the mice followed him and again he went ashore, but at last was overtaken by them and perished.

The other legend refers to Rudesheim. In the early days of the Crusades there lived a preacher, Bernard of Clairvoix. He exhorted his people to the great cause, and among those who obeyed his summons, was Knight Bromser, of Rudesheim, a widower, and father of a beautiful daughter, who was very dear to him. Bromser owned a fine castle in the Rhine valley and was rich and much esteemed, and the only regret he had in leaving home, was his daughter Gisela, whom he did not wish to expose to danger, but his desire to fight for the right prevailed, and he left his home accompanied by the tears and blessings of his child. Arriving at his post, he was recognized as a brave man, and charged with many commands that required valor. In this rocky, mountainous country, not far from the camp, came their water supply, which one day ceased, and it was found the cause was a terrible fiery dragon that had chosen this place for his home. The Emperor Conrad, who commanded the army, sought in vain for help, until one day Bromser offered his services and, accompanied by the blessings of all, started on his perilous errand, and after a long combat, killed the dragon. Glad at his success, he was preparing to return, when he was surrounded by a number of Saracens and taken prisoner, and he was confined in a dungeon, where he was seized with a desire for his native home and his child. In this condition he made a vow that if he was allowed to return home, he would found a convent and dedicate his daughter as the first nun. One dark night the Crusaders attacked the castle, released the knight and in due season he returned home, where his daughter met him joyfully.

The day after Bromser's arrival, a young knight, Kurt of Falkenstein, presented himself and told how he had met Gisela and won her love, and only required a father's blessing. Bromser in sorrow was obliged to refuse, as he would otherwise willingly have consented, for he knew the young knight's father, who was a favorite companion in arms. He told Kurt of his vow, who, after hearing the story, rushed in madness from the room, mounted his charger and hastened away. Meanwhile Gisela fell to the ground insensible, and from that hour was deranged, and one night bade her father farewell, and threw herself into the Rhine. The father's life was full of grief. He built the convent, and one day a farm servant brought him a wooden cross which was turned up in ploughing; on this spot he built a church and, to this day, the place has been regarded as a Mecca for those who were sick or in distress.

So much for the legends of the Rhine.

At 8:45 P. M. we arrived at Biebrich, where we boarded the train and in half an hour were at Frankfort-on-the-Main.

The Captain expressed his satisfaction with the day's journey, but was still inclined to be a little cross, because of his utter failure to get an oyster stew and a piece of apple pie for dinner, and that President McKinley was taken for an Irishman.

CHAPTER VII.

In Fatherland.

LEAVING the Rhine we stopped over a short while at our landing place, Biebrich, with nothing of importance to relate, except an incident that drew my attention to the fact that the Germans were very anxious to become familiar with the English language, which is now taught to a great extent in their public schools. I was standing near the station when I noticed a bright-faced, clean cut young fellow, perhaps 25 years old. I approached him and asked "Sprechen sie Englisch?"

"A leedle," was his reply.

I got in conversation with him, after a fashion, and he asked me if I thought he would learn English.

"Keep it up and you will get there," was my answer.

"Vot vas dot?" he asked.

"Keep it up," I returned.

"Keepd her upd, who vas he?"

I explained to his satisfaction "who he was," and he gratefully turned to me and said:

"I dink so. English vas more sphoken now as id vas sphoken py dose vot sphoke id, put feefty years ago French vas more sphoken py dose vot all sphoke it."

I came near asking him "Vot vas dot?" but I rather think I pleased him when I replied that he was correct.

We soon found ourselves at Frankfort-on-the-Main, one of the finest cities in Germany. In fact, in my opinion, it stands next to Berlin. Frankfort has a population of 230,000. This is an important commercial center and has fine streets and buildings. There are not many public buildings or galleries to attract the tourist's attention. This is more of a manufacturing center. The Old Bridge, built in 1342, crosses the Main and has a modern statue of Charlemagne. The town hall or Romer House was built in the fifteenth century and

Mosaic Beds in the Palm Garden, Frankfort.

is of historical note. Here is the electors' room where they used to assemble. In the Kaisersaal or Kings' room are life size portraits of all the kings from Charles the Great to Francis the Second (768 to 1792). In the Romer all the kings were elected. In front stands the Justitia Fountain, originally erected in 1611, afterward ruined and copied and restored May 10, 1887. It is said that in olden times when a king was elected, wine was used in the fountain instead of water.

At 11 Romerberg was the house in which Queen Louise lived. She was the wife of Frederick the Fourth, first Emperor of Germany, and mother of William the First, and great-grandmother of the present Emperor. The house where Goethe was born in 1749 is at 23 Grosser Hirschgraben. There is a house in the Domplatz where Luther stopped in 1521. Other places of note are the Domkirche or Cathedral built in 1346, and fine monuments to Schiller and Goethe. Here is also located the finest palm garden it has been my good fortune to have ever visited. There are many fine art stores here, where only the best class of works are sold. The display of palms, flowers, etc., is simply gorgeous.

It was here at Frankfort that I informed the Captain that at our next stopping place, Heidelberg, we would visit the ruins of the finest old castle in Germany.

"Well," he replied, "you can go and see it if you want to. I didn't come over here to see castles."

"What did you come for?" I asked.

"For fun," was his reply.

And the Captain took off his hat and mopped his brow with his handkerchief.

The story of Frankfort's foundation, as shown by a legend, gives this honor to Charlemagne, who fought against the Saxons with the fortunes of war often unfavorable to him. A brave, liberty-loving people often gave him powerful resistance, and he was often repelled by their superiority. It was in one of these encounters that he was obliged to retire before them on the banks of the Main. A thick fog covered the river and it was impossible to find a vessel to afford Charles and his army a passage. It was while he was pondering on what to do, that a deer with her young one, alarmed at the approach of the soldiers, sprang out of the thicket and waded with her through

The Palm Garden, Frankfort.

the river. Charles took advantage of this without delay and followed her course with his army and escaped from the enemy. Arriving on the other bank, Charles was so full of gratitude that he struck his spear into the sand and declared that here a town should rise and be called Frankenford, in memory of the event. Later on, when he overthrew the Saxons, he founded Frankfort, which later became so celebrated for the imperial coronations.

The Römer is remembered in legend. There was a great masked ball at one of the coronation festivals, and the rich salon was all aglow with the festive princes and knights. With a single exception each one present was filled with the gaiety of the occasion, and he was a tall knight clad in deep black armor, who attracted the attention of all. Who was he? None could guess. Toward the latter part of the evening he approached the Empress, knelt before her and asked the pleasure of a waltz. She consented, and with light and graceful steps he glided along the great salon with his sovereign, who thought she had never before enjoyed such a dance. At the end of the waltz he begged a second, a third and a fourth dance, which the Empress gladly accorded him, and he was envied by many a gallant knight, who would have considered even one dance from Her Majesty a personal favor, and consequently the curiosity of those present was increased to know who he was, even the Emperor sharing in the excitement. At last the hour arrived when each one who was masked must make himself or herself known. All unmasked except the stranger, who refused, when in desperation the Emperor commanded him to do so. Then he lifted his visor. None knew him. Two officials at last advanced and, as they gazed upon him, beheld the executioner of Bergen, when, glowing with rage, the Emperor commanded that he be seized and led to death, as he had disgraced the Empress and insulted the crown.

The executioner saw that he had displeased all, and especially his King and Queen, so going before them he threw himself on his knees and admitted that he had not only committed a great wrong but had disgraced his sovereign, so gaining the King's attention he told him that even death was not a fit punishment, and as it would not help the case, suggested as a remedy that the King draw his sword and then and there knight him, and he would thereafter throw down his gauntlet to anyone who dared speak disrespectfully of the King or

The Conservatory, Palm Garden, Frankfort.

Queen. The King made up his mind this was the wisest course to pursue, and drawing his sword said : "Arise, Knave of Bergen, knave you have been, knave you shall be," and the black knight arose amid the applause of all present.

While at Frankfort, I became acquainted with a German official, who was much interested in America and Americans. In conversing with him one afternoon, the Captain came up, and I introduced him, and, in true Yankee style, the Captain immediately inquired of him his business.

"I am connected," he replied, "with the Great German Empire ; and your profession, if you please?"

"Well," replied the Captain, as he put his hands in his pockets, "I am connected with the Stars and Stripes, the greatest flag that ever floated to the breezes."

And the Captain turned his back on us and walked down the corridor of the hotel.

From Frankfort we passed on to the famous university town of Heidelberg. As I walked through its quaint streets and passed around the university building, it recalled my boyhood days when I enjoyed reading Ralph Keeler's work, "A Tour of Europe for $80 in Currency." It was to Heidelberg that Keeler came, and here by dint of hard work he managed to secure an education. Keeler was a famous minstrel in after years.

Heidelberg is located on the left bank of the Neckar, and has a population of about 60,000. Four streets course the town, with numerous side streets leading from them. Of the population about three-fifths are Protestants and two-fifths Catholics. Over 1100 students reside here, which gives life to the town. It is said that among all the German universities that at Heidelberg is the most renowned for its original student life. This is the home of dueling practice, and nearly every day there are scientific fencing exhibitions. The University was erected in 1711. It stands on the spot once occupied by the ancient Augustine monastery, where Luther, as deputy, stood before the court of Augustine monks, April 26, 1518, and defended before priests, students and the people his religion. Probably the most interesting place is the old cancer, or students' prison. The floor is plated and the walls blackened by the smoke of lamps. Here the students were confined for misdemeanors. The longest time on

The Old Castle, Heidelberg.

record for which anyone has been locked up, is forty-four days, while the shortest time is one day. The room is without furniture, and the windows iron grated. The new cancer is what the students call "a jolly prison" compared with the old one, and consists of several cells in the third story of the building, and the whole is covered with caricatures drawn on the walls by students who were confined there. While I remarked that this building was erected in the past century, the university was founded in 1386, and was the third one in the German empire. It has a library of 380,000 volumes and about 165,000 pamphlets, and in hand writing 3334 codices, 2495 deeds and 2512 charters.

In the market place is the old house known as Hans zum Ritter, now used as a restaurant. It is built in style of the Renaissance, and was completed by Huguenot Belier in 1592. The facade with sharp gable and two attics is richly decorated with statues and ornaments, and on the top are portraits of four Franconian kings, and in the center are portraits of the builder and his wife with their coat of arms, and below them their two children and two rams. Opposite this old house is the Holy Ghost Church, with a lot of stands and shops for business purposes erected all along the under side. This church is remarkable for the fights that have been made for its possession by the Protestants and Catholics, and is at the present time used by both denominations for religious purposes. The church was erected in 1398-1414. Catholic services were held here until the reign of Frederic II., when on Sunday, Dec. 20, 1545, the first Protestant services were held. Karl V. prohibited this, and Otto Heinrich restored it in 1556, and various changes were made as years rolled on, until 1705 when a partition was put up between the aisles, and one-half given to each denomination, and to that use it is made to this day.

While here, I was late at my dinner one day and entered the dining room just as the Captain was passing out.

"Well," I remarked to the Captain, "what kind of a dinner did you have today?"

"Oh," replied the Captain, "very fair indeed ; they had two kinds."

"Two kinds of what?" I asked.

"Well," he replied, "a table de hotey and an alley carte."

Students Fencing at Heidelberg.

Just then two American ladies passed us and I was undecided whether to take my dinner in the dining room, or repair to some restaurant.

The attraction of Heidelberg is the old castle ruins, which show off in majestic splendor from the top of a high hill at the extreme further end of the town, and said to be the finest and most picturesque old ruins in Germany. The first early knowledge of the place dates from 1303. Arriving at the top of the hill, which is reached by either a carriage drive or an inclined railway, we enter a magnificent garden surrounding the ruins. This is now known as the garden of Ludwig V., but was formerly called the Grand Rampart. I visited the old ruins six years ago, but vast improvements have been made since that time in the grounds that surround it.

The view of Heidelberg and the surrounding country from the lofty gardens surrounding the castle is beyond description and well worth a visit here to see. Entering the gateway of the castle, on the left we find the glass hall erected by Frederic II., built four stories high. The vaulted galleries are easily recognized, in the three rows of arcades resting upon stout Doric columns. This hall was destroyed in 1689. To the eastward is the Otto Heinrich building, the grand facade plainly showing its imitation of the Italian renaissance. This is considered the finest piece of architecture of the whole building. The plan was made by Frederic II., and completed by Heinrich in his short reign of only three years. The upper part of the nterior of the castle is wholly destroyed, only two single columns remain. The Otto Heinrich building is connected with the glass hall and just in front is the Zeughaus, built by Frederic II., in 1549. The Bell Tower comes next, and was built by Frederick the Victorious. A stone stairway leads to the top, where a fine view of the old ruins, as well as the town, can be seen. There are other connections with this old castle galore. I could use half a dozen pages in describing them. Take my advice, and if you ever have the opportunity, go see them. I have been there twice and could enjoy another visit. I must not, however, forget to mention that in the cellar are the two great wine casks of renown, holding 15,000 and 30,000 gallons respectively, and opposite the larger one is a carved figure of Clemens Perkes, the dwarf from Tyrol, Court Jester of Karl Phillip. Perkes, although small of stature, was large of thirst, for he is said to have consumed on an average fifteen to eighteen bottles of wine daily.

Heidelberg University.

Bowing is not only a habit but a science in Heidelberg. Everybody bows and such a bow! The hat is lifted and brought down at an angle with the right leg. One evening we were going into the concert garden—the Captain and myself—and as we passed up to buy our ticket, the ticket-seller took off his cap to us. I bowed in return, while the Captain looked on. As we were passing out near the close of the performance, the same individual saw us coming down the path and lifted his cap again, while I returned the salute. Turning to me the Captain remarked, "Where did you get acquainted with that duffer?" When I told him of the custom, he vowed he would not forget it, and sure enough he did not, for the next day a regiment of soldiers passed our hotel from a camping, and as the commander rode up on his horse, the captain took off his hat, and the salute was returned in a like manner. "There," remarked the Captain, "when I bow, I bow to a person of importance, not a ticket-seller in a concert garden."

When stopping at a hotel on the Continent, the tourist should remember and make a price in advance to include room, light and attendance, or an extra charge will be made. It is also necessary to provide your own soap, as this is always charged extra. Another little item of expense, that would seem exorbitant in the United States, is, whenever you go to a theater, concert or place of amusement, you are obliged to pay for a program, and if you want a railroad time table on the Continent you must pay for that also.

From Heidelberg we made our journey on to Wurtzburg, a quaint old city of 50,000 population, and the home of the famous Wurtzburg Hoffbrau beer. At the upper end of the main street there was a sight for us well worth going a long way. For a half a mile this street was extended in the shape of a bazar, both sides being lined with booths where everything from a horseshoe nail to a brass watch could be obtained. At the extreme end were flying horses, target galleries, swings, side shows, etc., the whole resembling the outskirts of a country fair, or a miniature Midway Plaisance.

During our visit at Wurtzburg, I made a tour of the place to purchase some cigars and traveled the whole town over to find one at twenty pfennigs (five cents) each, the usual price being from one to three cents, American money. I was complaining to the Captain about my inability to secure a good smoke here and that the cigars were sold at so low a figure.

The Great Wine Cask, Heidelberg.

"That reminds me," he remarked, "if I remember rightly, I promised you two boxes of cigars, if you would make this tour with me."

I shuddered, as I informed him he was correct. Nothing further was thought of the matter until that night when, after dinner, the Captain passed over to me two boxes, each containing fifty cigars.

"There," he remarked. "this pays my debt to you, and you will find here as good a smoke as you ever had."

Timidly, I inquired of the Captain, if I might be so ungallant as to ask him how much he paid per box for the cigars.

"Certainly," was his reply, "they cost me just four marks per box."

That meant just one dollar in American money, or two cents each. Need I say that before I departed from Wurtzburg, the porter of the hotel owned the two boxes of cigars?

CHAPTER VIII.

Nuremberg and Munich.

WHILE we were at one of the way stations on our way to Nuremberg, the Captain had occasion to make a slight purchase. The attendant who waited upon him spoke English, so the Captain had no trouble in securing what he wanted. After the purchase was completed, he passed over in payment, an American silver dollar; the clerk looked it over for an instant, and turning to my friend remarked:

'This is American money."

"Well," answered the Captain, "what if it is? I am an American."

And in the hot sun of a summer afternoon, I left the depot, wondering if there was not at times a good excuse for crime.

"You are now to see the most unique city in Germany," remarked a gentleman to me, as our train neared Nuremberg, or, as it is called in German, Nurnberg.

I must acknowledge he was right, and that Nuremberg is well called, "The City of the Middle Ages." In size it is the second largest in Bavaria, and has a population of 175,000. The old city was until 1848 surrounded by a wall, with eight gates leading into the town. The wall still remains and the number of gates has been increased to seventeen. With the advancement of population and improvements, the city's size has increased beyond the enclosure, and the best portion, or new buildings, are outside of it. The city is divided by the river Pegnitz, and six stone bridges cross the same. The present appearance of the old part is mediæval, and in order to preserve all the old and original appearances, repairs and restorations are carried out in the old German or Gothic style. The streets are irregular, and many alleys or byways connect some of the leading thoroughfares.

Nuremberg is quite a manufacturing center. Here are made the celebrated Faber lead pencils, and there are many other industries for which this section is noted. In addition to this, here is the principal home and export market for hops, which are grown throughout all this Bavarian country.

The history of the city dates back from 1050, over 800 years ago. In 1105 Heinrich V. took and destroyed the town, and in 1127 the Emperor Lothar conquered the city. Emperor Konrad III., who did much toward improving the town, lived here in 1147, and Frederic I. Barbarossa, who enlarged the castle, lived here on and off between 1156 and 1188. From this period on to the sixteenth century, when the town was in its prime, various monarchs held and lost their sway here. In these times were born and lived here men like Albert Durer, the greatest of German painters, Hans Sachs, the famous poet-shoemaker, and others of equal note.

Toward the middle of the sixteenth century, the effects of doubling the Cape of Good Hope had a serious result on the business of the city, as the trade of Nuremberg with Vienna and the Netherland cities began to decline. The building of the town hall was the last great effort of the government, while the Thirty Years' War fully exhausted the last means of the town, and killed its commerce. In this condition it was practically helpless, and it was fortunate to be able to incorporate into the Kingdom of Bavaria in 1806. Maximilian I., did much to improve the city, and under the reign of Ludwig II., the city began to rise and prosper. During the war of 1866, the city was occupied by the Prussian troops under the Duke of Mecklenburg, and from that date on to the present, prosperity and happiness have attended the old city.

It is not within my province to give such a description of the city, as it now stands (I refer to the old part) that would do it justice. There are many attractions in the town—old churches, the Old Castle, Hangman's Bridge, monuments, Bavarian Industrial Museum, German National Museum, the City Hall, Albert Durer's house, and other minor affairs. I will briefly tell the story of what interested me most.

First, the Old Castle, the most interesting part of which was the five cornered tower, where is stored a great display of instruments used during the Inquisition, a full description of each being given by a guide in attendance. Several floors are devoted to this collection, while the top floor contains a fine display of old armor, musical instruments, articles of warfare, etc.

Maximilian Palace from the River Isra, Nuremberg.

It was here that the Captain called my attention to a piece of armor of the fourteenth century, with the foot covering extending to a sharp point. "There," he remarked, "is the origin of the razor toe shoe," and I was half inclined to believe that some of our Yankee shoe manufacturers had been over here and got a pointer for a new style.

Passing from this section, we go to the old well-room, where a curiosity awaits our arrival. This well, which is about six feet in diameter, is 335 feet deep. The attendant filled a large beer glass with water, emptied its contents into the well, and it was just six seconds before we heard the splash as it reached the bottom. Another glassful of water was emptied at six intervals, and after the last had left the glass, each of the six splashes was distinctly heard as it fell. A box about fifteen inches square, with glass sides, and containing four or five lighted candles, was lowered 300 feet, and, with the aid of a mirror at the top, the bottom could be very distinctly seen. The well was cut in rock by prisoners who were confined here in the eleventh century, under Konrad II. It took thirty years to finish it. A subterranean passage leads from near the bottom of the well to the town hall, and another formerly led to St. John, a suburb. The latter has, however, been destroyed.

The castle contains many apartments, in a fine state of preservation. At the time I visited it, workmen were engaged in restoring certain parts. In the Knights' Hall are to be seen some fine old German paintings. There is also an interesting double chapel, built in the romantic style of the twelfth century. The stoves, made of tile and mammoth in size, are real curiosities, yet stoves of a like description are used the present day in all the leading public and private buildings of Germany. In the courtyard is an old lime tree, planted by the Empress Kunigunda in 1002, nearly 900 years ago.

The Rathaus, or town hall, is a splendid specimen of the old Renaissance in early Italian style. One painting that covers one-half of the entire side, is "The Triumphal Procession of the Emperor Maximilian," by the pupils of Alfred Durer and after his own style.

It was the second day after our arrival in Nuremberg, and while at dinner, that the Captain thought he had a good one on me. The day was warm, and I ordered a bottle of Munich beer. When the waiter brought it on, I protested and declared it was not Munich. He de-

clared it was, but I afterward found I was right. The bottle was of ordinary size and, when I came to settle for it, was charged two marks or fifty cents. Again I protested, and said it was an exorbitant charge to make, so the head waiter was called in to settle the dispute. When he heard the story, he turned to me and said, " If you want to drink beer for dinner, go over in that room where this much will cost you twenty pfennigs (five cents); here you must drink wine or pay wine prices." This pleased the Captain to that extent that he nearly choked from laughter. He said it was well worth ten dollars to him to see some one get the best of me.

St. Lawrence Church is an interesting old cathedral, originally built 900 years ago. It is supported by 26 pillars and is 322 feet long by 104 feet wide, and 104 feet high. The handsomest part of the church is the choir, with its vaulted roof, supported with slender pillars from which the arches spring like palm branches. The seven windows here are the bert examples of old Nuremberg glass painting, dating from 1450. The representations are the "Last Supper" and the "Wanderings of the Children of Israel," the "Story of the Passion" and the "Transfiguration." One represents the donor, the Emperor Frederic and his wife. Memorial coats of arms of patrician families hang in groups on the pillars and in the chapels, while the tapestries on the walls represent the lives of St. Lawrence and St. Catharine, and are over 400 years old. There are many paintings of note. This church, originally a Catholic cathedral, has for years been a Protestant house of worship, although all the old altars and emblems of ages ago still remain as when formerly used.

We, the Captain and myself, had passed a day full of sight-seeing, and after our dinner we were enjoying a cigar in the smoking room, when I asked my friend how he was impressed with what he had seen thus far in Europe.

"Which way?" replied the Captain.

"Why, the strange people we meet, the customs and ways, and all this confusion, does it not impress you?"

"Yes," answered the Captain, "it does."

"Well," I asked, "what way?"

"The thing that most impressed me," was his reply, "is that, in all our tour, I have not found an oyster stew on a single bill of fare."

And the Captain continued to smoke his cigar in peace while I was forced to drown my sorrow in the thought that even the good have their punishment here below.

The most noted church in Nuremberg, is St. Sebaldus, finished in the tenth century. Here is to be seen a font, remarkable as one of the first products of one of the industries of the town, as well as having served to christen King Wenzeslas of Bohemia on the 11th of April, 1361. In the column of the pulpit is an original painting by Alfred Durer, the "Interment of Jesus," while opposite is a copy of Rubens' "The Day of Judgment." Other paintings by Durer and artists of celebrity are shown. The eastern choir of the church is built in genuine gothic style, decorated with fine columns and completed in 1377. In the center of the choir is the sepulchre of St. Sebaldus. This is the most celebrated of German monuments and was cast by Peter Vischen and his five sons, begun in 1508 and completed in 1519. It rests on twelve snails, supposed to represent the slow progress of the world. Four dolphins adorn the corners, the whole forming a temple, adorned with the twelve apostles, and this is surmounted by twelve smaller figures, being as many fathers of the church, and finally by an infant Christ holding a globous in his hand.

There are a number of altars, paintings by celebrated artists and an organ built in 1444 and renovated in 1821. The exterior of the church, on the north side, has what is called the Bridal Door, with statues of the five wise and five foolish virgins. Originally built as a Roman Catholic Cathedral, the first Protestant services were held here in 1530 and since that period, it has been used by this denomination. Like St. Lawrence Church, all the old altars and choirs used when the church was first erected, still remain.

From Nuremberg we journeyed on to Munich, or as they call it in Germany, Munchen, the largest city in Baravia, and with a population of about 420,000. Here we find quite a military center, and withal a beautiful city, modern in every sense, and with a people well-to-do and wide awake. This is the home of the Munich beer, known the world over as the finest brewed malt beer that is made. There is considerable manufacturing, including bronze works. The streets are wide, well laid out and kept clean, while many monuments of elaborate description adorn public squares.

While here, the Captain asked me one day, as we were strolling along the street, if I knew the German for hot water. I told him it was "Heisses Wasser," and asked him why he wanted to know. His reply was, that he was going in to get a shave, and he wanted the barber to use hot water. So presently we came to a barber shop and entered. Taking off his hat, the Captain beckoned to the attendant, and gesticulating that he wanted a shave, exclaimed "Heisses Wasser." The barber nodded, went at his work and never said a word until he got ready to clean his face when, taking a sponge, he remarked in good English, "Would you like some warm water on your face?" The Captain looked up, and when he found he had the best shave since his arrival in Europe he asked the man where he learned English, and was surprised to find he had resided in New York for eight years, was a naturalized American citizen and his wife an American women. The Captain paid an extra price for that shave.

Munich is one of the art centers of Europe. Here is located Old Pinakothek and the New Pinakothek, both galleries of a world wide reputation. One contains the works of old masters, while the other those of modern masters. There is a so a permanent exhibition of art, etc., and many elegant art stores. Many pictures are sold here to go to the United States, and in ninety-nine cases out of a hundred the purchaser pays a profit of at least 75 per cent of the purchase price. The gallery contains many paintings of remarkable beauty. At the New Pinakothek my attention was drawn to Carl Von Piloty's "Seni before Wallenstein's Corpse," and "Thusnelda in the Triumphal Train of Germanicus." Also "The Deluge" by Carl Schoon, and "The Destruction of Jerusalem" by Wilhelm Von Kaulbach. All through these great galleries is seen the hand of the master in art, and to study them carefully would take weeks.

The old Church of St. Michael is a beautiful piece of architecture of the Italian style, built in 1488. It is in a good state of preservation, and used regularly for services. There are numbers of other churches here that will well repay a visit.

Here is also located the Royal Bronze Foundry. open for inspection from 1 to 6 P. M., to those who are interested. Among the works turned out here is the statue of Bavaria and the beautiful fountain at Cincinnati, Ohio. The colossal statue of Bavaria and her Lion is erected on a hill outside the Sendlinger Thor, in the Theresienwiese. It is of copper, 60 feet high, and rests on a pedestal 40 feet high. A stairway leads to the top, and the head will hold six persons.

Karlsbridge, with St. Sebolds Church, Nuremberg.

The second largest library in the world, the Royal Library, is located here. It is richly appointed, and contains 1,200,000 volumes and 25,000 manuscripts. There is also another one here containing 300,000 books. One could easily spend a week or more in Munich in sight seeing. In the season this is a great operatic center, and the best talent in the world is brought here. During the summer season fine concerts are given in halls and gardens.

One evening while we were in this city, we were approached by the head waiter of our hotel, who asked us if we did not want to attend the Harmonic Society's Concert?

"What is that?" remarked the Captain.

"Probably what you call the Symphony," was the reply.

So the Captain immediately bought two tickets and we wended our way and attended one of the finest concerts we had the pleasure of hearing while in Europe. On our return to our hotel, I asked the Captain how he enjoyed the evening.

"I was very much disappointed," was his reply.

"How so?" I asked.

"Well," was his reply, "out of fifty musicians, I did not see a single one playing the harmonica, and when I bought those tickets, I bought them for a Sympathy Concert, supposing it was to benefit some poor person, but from the way things were carried on, I imagine it was a money-making scheme," and just then the moon went down behind a cloud and I felt relieved.

I suppose the place that interested me most of all was the Royal Palace, positively, thus far, the finest and largest I had inspected. This building consists of three main parts, the old and the new residence or the Konigsbau, and the Festsaalbau or state apartments. They are all connected, as is also the court chapel and the two court theaters. The court or old palace was built by Maximilian I., and commenced in 1600 and finished 1616; the original size was 180x90. It is in the Renaissance. The two Doric doors are covered with rich embellishments. Entering into the chapel court, the old chapel is situated at the right, while in the vaulted passage leading from this to the court of the fountain lies a stone that weighs 364 pounds. This stone was lifted and thrown a great distance by Herzog Christolph, son of Albert III.

Close to it in the wall are three nails, one above the other, and the story goes that young Herzog knocked off the upper one, which is

Hangman's Bridge, Nuremberg.

twelve feet from the ground, with a blow of his foot ; the second, six and one-half feet from the ground, was knocked down in a like manner by Conrad, and the third, eight and one-half feet from the ground, by Philip the Springer. There is an old tablet on the wall bearing these words : "Whoever jumps higher will be removed." A door to the right leads into the grotto courts with a small garden, embellished with fountains, etc. The most important apartments on the first story, are those of Charles VII., including the dining room and audience hall, with portraits of the twelve Roman Emperors. On the ground floor is the treasury, with a wealth of good things in the way of fine old portraits. jewels, etc., worn by kings and queens, princes and princesses. The rich chapel has a floor of mosaic. A multitude of jewels, gold and silver vessels, beautiful embossed work in precious metals, relics of the saints, etc., are kept here. A particularly interesting work of art is a "Descent from the Cross " done in raised wax by Michael Angelo.

The new palace was built in 1826 by command of King Ludwig I. Its front is 140 meters (or about 455 feet) long. The apartments are finely furnished. There are bedrooms, ante-rooms, dining-rooms and public and private reception rooms. The halls are adorned with elegant tapestries and paintings in oil.

The state department or Festsaalbau, is 820 feet long. This splendid building was commenced in 1832 and finished in 1842 and is of the Venetian style. The arches statues and arabesques are representations of Bavarian history, while the adornment of the grand halls is beyond description. The paintings, tapestries, ornamentations and furniture are simply grand. The Throne Room is 118 meters long, and 25 meters wide, with side galleries, each supported by ten Corinthian columns, and between them stand twelve colossal figures in rich gilt bronze, representing the ancestors of the house of Wittelsbach. Indeed, this fine palace is a most interesting place.

The Schack Gallery is small, but interesting. The ceiling of the first saloon is done from copies of Michael Angelo. This gallery is in the house of Count Schack. He died in 1894 and bequeathed this collection to the German Emperor, who afterward bought the count's house and left the collection here.

While at Munich, the opera was on and one night, I asked the Captain how he would like to go and see the "Barber of Seville."

Ludwigstrasse, Munich.

"You could not have asked me in a better time," was his reply, "I was going to try to shave myself, but find my razor is dull, so I will gladly accompany you."

The National Museum is a magnificent building, and one of the richest in point of collections in Europe. All the antique treasures formerly scattered about in royal palaces and other places throughout Bavaria, have been gathered together here, and placed in one grand collection.

A visit to the Royal Bronze Foundry will fairly make an American tourist rise up in his might and shout for joy. Entering the model room or, as it is called, the museum, which contains full size sculptors' casts of many celebrated statues, etc., almost the first sight that meets one's eye is the cast of the great Emancipation statue, erected in Boston, and just beyond it, is the cast of the heroic statue of Washington, erected in Baltimore. There are many other casts of American statesmen. At the base of the Washington cast were nearly one thousand personal cards of American visitors, who had deposited them there while visiting the works. Mine went in with the rest and the Captain insisted on going up to the hotel and getting a large half sheet poster of the Emerson shoe and leaving that as a memento, but I finally made him understand this could not be allowed, so he deposited his card calling for 29 shoe stores.

While at Munich one could make an interesting trip and visit the favorite castles of the late King Ludwig II. Berg is the smallest and is located on the Lake of Starnberg. The interior is simple and the rooms are small when compared with the others. It was here the king passed his last hours.

Herrenchiernsee Castle is located on Herren Island. It is two stories high and 100 meters long. The building and grounds are finely appointed and the decorations and fittings of the castle are fine.

Neuschwanstein Castle is located about one hour's walk from the the village of Fussen. The principal apartment is the Throne Room, a great hall in the byzantine style and two stories high. High marble columns support two galleries, one above the other. The dining-room is in red and gold, while the other apartments are fine. The whole is rich in paintings and decorations.

Linderhof Castle is near Oberau, and while the building is not to be seen for any distance, it is an old structure, however. The chief

beauty here is the magnificent gardens. The castle itself is only one story and small in dimensions. The Gobelin Room furniture is covered with real Gobelin embroidery and the wall ornamented with paintings in the Gobelin style. The Yellow Cabinet is finished with yellow silk and gold embroidery. The Violet Cabinet in violet and gold. The Rose and Blue Cabinet in rose and blue. In the gardens all is magnificence and splendor and must be seen to be appreciated.

So we closed our visit to Munich and the Captain asked me where we were next bound for. When I told him Switzerland, he offered to bet me $10 its scenery could not stand a show beside that of the White Mountains or California.

During our stay here there was some kind of a national celebration going on, and the Captain and I started out in the afternoon to take in the sights. Our attention was attracted to a hurdy-gurdy, playing the "Star Spangled Banner." It interested the Captain to that extent that he kept within hearing distance of the organ, until it had finished the piece. Arriving at the market-place, we found a band concert in progress, and the populace were loud in their cheers of the national anthems. It was while I listened to this music, I missed the Captain and hunted in every direction for him, until I finally made up my mind, he had either got lost, or had gone back to the hotel. I started in that direction, when you can imagine my surprise to see him coming up the street with the man with the hurdy-gurdy following. Knowing that something was in the wind, I crossed to the opposite side and watched the Captain plant his man with the hurdy-gurdy in front of the brass band, and after a few gestures to him, the man started up the "Star Spangled Banner." What the result was, I cannot say, but I made a bee line for the hotel and left the Captain to face the consequences. At the same time, as the Captain returned to the hotel in good condition, I have every reason believe that the general public of Nuremberg did not know the American National Anthem.

CHAPTER IX.

Our First Week in Switzerland.

THE Captain wanted to bet me $10 that the White Mountain scenery would surpass that of Switzerland. I even believe that after passing through the latter country, the Captain would make this bet regarding his own native heath, Bethel, Me., but the Captain is not a lover of nature.

From Munich we entered Switzerland, our first stopping place being Zurich. We came down by way of Landau and crossed Lake Constance. With the exception of the lake ride, the journey is uneventful of scenery of a mountainous nature, yet there is an interesting panorama of rustic life well worth the trip. But as regards Swiss mountain scenery, in my opinion there is no more comparison between that of Switzerland and the White Mountains, than there could be between the Hudson river and the Atlantic ocean. Both are vastly different, and Switzerland leads the world in this particular gift of nature.

Zurich, the metropolis of Switzerland, is a beautiful city of 150,000 population, and lies on the lake of the same name and at the point where the river Limmat starts its course. The city extends from the heights of Zurichberg to the base of the steep ridge, called the Uto. Its importance is partly owing to its situation at the foot of the Alps, and 1345 feet above sea level. It is also on the ancient commercial highway leading from the heart of Lombardy, across the mountains of Rhaetia, and along the various lakes and rivers into Germany. The walks and rides through the suburbs are fine, the woods and paths are well kept, and the variety of scenery beautiful. The hotel where we stopped, the Baur-au-lac, or "Bower by the lake," faces the lake, with a magnificent garden of walks, trees and shrubbery in front, which extend to the lake front. In the evening, when the house and gardens shine with hundreds of lights, and the city part of the lake front glows with the same, the scene is like that of fairyland. Looking beyond, we find both sides of this sheet of water lined with villas, typical of Swiss architecture, while the waters glitter with the little crafts that are gliding here and there. Steamboats course the lake constantly, and visit many interesting points, including Au and quiet Ufenau, which Conrad Meyer has so poetically woven in his beautiful song of "Hutton's Last Days."

The attractions in Zurich are noble churches with ancient history attached, the town library of 130,000 volumes, the Antiquarian Museum, the Town Hall, the Swiss National Museum, schools and universities and other public buildings.

It was while we were at Zurich that the Captain's attention was attracted to a poster of a "circus," admission ten francs ($2), and he was determined to visit the "show," so he started out to find the place, and at last succeeded and paid his money. But when he entered the building he was rather taken back by being addressed in English, and asked what kind of a horse he preferred. The Captain turned to me to help him out, and upon inquiry it was discovered that this "circus" was a school for horseback riding. The Captain refused to select a horse, left in disgust and the last I saw of him he was trying to find a soda fountain.

From Zurich we journeyed to Lucerne—Lucerne the beautiful. It was an easy place to reach, but a hard place to leave, because one feels like settling down in this spot. From the windows of my hotel I had a full view of the Rigi-Kulm and Pilatus, two mountains of note, while in all directions the vast chain, a part of the Alps, looms up before the eye. Here is where Swiss mountain scenery begins.

Lucerne has only 20,000 population, yet this number is swelled fifty per cent in the season. This is a summer resort pure and simple. The large hotels and many of the stores are closed from October to April. The town lies directly on the Lake of Lucerne, one of the finest sheets of water in all Europe. The old walls, which once encircled the town, are in part intact, and from the lake command a unique view. The inhabitants still cling to the mediæval usages and frolics of carnival time, yet all is changed in the summer season. When we arrived here, and were on our way to the hotel, it was a question with me if Lucerne was not a part of the United States, for the Star Spangled Banner floated in all directions, from buildings, in store

Zurich from the Lake.

windows and on the boats on the lake. But, alas! it was only a
scheme to catch dollars from the Yankee visitors. When we walked
the streets and entered public places, stores, etc., it seemed to me that
all with whom we came in contact spoke English, but when we entered the old cathedral to attend the organ concert, and an admission
fee of one franc was charged, it was a case of a decidedly foreign
aspect. By the way, speaking of these organ concerts, which are a
feature here and take place every evening at 6:30, one who is a lover
of music will find a rare treat in them. The organ was built in 1651
and remodeled in 1851.

It was here that the Captain thought he had got in trouble. He
entered a cigar store and bought one franc's worth, and tendered in
payment a gold ten franc piece, which he said was the smallest change
he had. In the meantime the attendant, who could not speak English, passed out nine francs change. But in order to help out the
Captain I offered him a franc piece, which he gave in payment for
his cigars, and returned the silver change and took his gold piece. In
the meantime we loitered around a few moments, looking at this and
that, and as we started to leave the store, the attendant suddenly
recollected that he had given the Captain nine francs in silver and
also returned the ten franc gold piece, so he wanted his silver returned. In vain we explained that he had already taken his silver,
but he was not satisfied. Just then the rain began to drop, and the
Captain darted out of the door and made a bee line for the hotel, leaving me to settle the affair, which I finally did by having him count up
the contents of the money drawer. When I returned to the hotel I
found the Captain interviewing the portier on fines and sentences in
cases of flimflam.

The origin of Lucerne is said to be veiled in the mists of antiquity.
In the days of the Romans it was a small fishing town. It was in 695
that the first cathedral and convent, that of St. Leodegar, was founded
here by Duke Wickard, of Swabia. About this time, on account of
its increasing commerce with Germany and Italy, Lucerne was rising
in importance and was purchased by King Rudolf, of Hapsburg. The
town remained but a short time under the rule of Austria, acquiring its
freedom in 1321 by a union with the Three Cantons, with whom it had
been in league for eighty years. Eleven years later, in 1332, Lucerne
threw off its last yoke and formally joined the confederacy and was

Lucerne and the Alps.

for a long time the ecclesiastical capital of Switzerland, as well as the gathering place of those whose mercenary conduct in selling their services to the best paying state or monarch, long made Switzerland's name a byword among the nations. A few patrician families exercised a more or less despotic sway over the remainder of the canton, until the intervention of Napoleon in 1803. At the time of the war of the Sonderbond or Separate League, 1845 to 1847, Lucerne was the seat of the seceding government under Siegwart-Muller. The fate of the League was decided by the battle of Gisikon on the 23d of November, 1847, and the following day Lucerne capitulated. Under the promulgation of the new constitution of 1848, Lucerne shared with Berne and Zurich the distinction of being a meeting place of the Federal Assembly.

Lucerne contains but few buildings of public interest, but owes its charm to its situation on that romantic lake that bears its name. The cathedral is an attractive old building, the original of which, I made mention, was built in 695 and afterward destroyed by fire. The present edifice was erected about the middle of the seventeenth century, and is consequently nearly 250 years old. There are a number of fine old paintings, altars and statues to be seen here. In the churchyard surrounding the cathedral are many interesting monuments.

"Look here," said the Captain, as he walked up to me, and helped himself to a cigar from my vest pocket, "even the waterfalls of Switzerland seem to be run in the interest of the Switzer, as they flow during the tourist season and strike in the winter, when they are little needed, and when there are no rich Yankees here to view their beauties," and then the Captain borrowed a match from a passer-by, and as he stood there puffing my Havana he remarked to a native Swiss, who did not understand a word of English, that it was "a fine day."

Just beyond the cathedral is the attraction of Lucerne in the way of a novelty, and that is "The Lion in the Rock," positively the grandest piece of work I ever saw in my life. Facing a pool of water, is a perpendicular rock, possibly 100 feet high and as many feet wide. It has a smooth surface and in the center is cut a representation of a lion. The great beast lies stretched in the agonies of death, a broken lance piercing his side while his paw rests on the Bourbon coat of

arms as a token that even in death he will not forsake his trust. A pool of water overshadowed by pines and maples, bears the reflection of this noble beast upon its surface. This work was executed by Lucus Ahorn, of Constance. It was after a model by Thorwaldsen and was completed in 1821. It is intended as a monument to commemorate the soldiers and officers of the Swiss Guard who to the number of eight hundred laid down their lives at the Tuileries in Paris in defense of King Louis XVI., on the 10th of August and 2d and 3d of September, 1792. Above the Lion, which is possibly 25 feet in length, appears this inscription : " The Faith and Valor of Switzerland." Beneath are engraved the names of its officers. The men who so bravely gave up their lives are, perhaps, to find a more lasting monument in the eloquent words of Carlyle : " Honor to you, brave men ; honorable pity, through long times ! Not martyrs are ye, and yet almost more. He was no king of yours, this Louis, and he forsook you like a king of shreds and patches ! Ye were but sold to him for some poor sixpence a day, yet would ye work for your wages, keep your plighted word. The work now was to die, and ye did it. Honor to you, O kinsmen ! and may the old Deutsch Biederkiet and Tapferkeit and valor, which is worth and truth, be they Swiss, be they Saxon, fail in no age. Not bastards, true born are these men, sons of the men of Sempach of Murten, who knelt but not to thee, O Burgundy! Let the traveler, as he passes through Lucerne, turn aside to look a moment at their monumental Lion ; not for Thorwaldsen's sake alone. Hewn out of solid rock, the figure rests there by the still waters of the lake, in lullaby of distant tinkiing ranz-des-vaches, the granite mountains dumbly keeping watch all round, and, though inanimate, speaks."

These are Carlyle's words, and his tribute of years gone by still rings out words of cheer to the Swiss patriot.

The Captain was full of enthusiasm when we started to view "The Lion in the Rock." He was a "lover of wild beasts" and wanted to see this one. He saw it—in disgust. After viewing it for a moment he turned to me and remarked : "Let's go ; it is only hewn out of rock." But I lingered to look at this wonderful monument, while the Captain took in a panorama at an admission price of fifty centimes.

Near the "Lion in the Rock," stands a small chapel, dedicated to the slain soldiers and bearing the inscription : "Peace to the Uncon-

Rigi-Kulm Railway, Near Lucerne.

quered." The interior of the chapel is hung with the banners and weapons of the Guard, and on the 10th of August of each year masses are said here for the repose of the souls of the dead. When this information was conveyed to me, the thought occurred—after over one hundred years what would become of their souls if mass was omitted?

To the left of the Lion is the entrance to the Glacier Garden, a magnificent memorial of the glacier epoch. This furnishes a striking picture of the glacier's movements in polishing the surface of the rocks immediately underneath. It is unique. This must be seen to be fully appreciated. Down in the Weinmarkt is an ancient fountain erected in 1481, and in its immediate vicinity will be found the old Council House built in 1660. Four bridges cross the River Reuss, which commences here from the lake. There is only one of real interest, and that is known as the Kopellbrucke, and is an old, dilapidated affair of considerable length. It is built of wood roofed in, and is for pedestrians only. The Kopellbrucke is over 700 years old, yet is still in daily use. The rafters are ornamented with a series of paintings called by some "The Dance of Death," although I was unable to find any authenticity for this, for they are generally supposed to represent scenes from the lives of St. Leodegar and Maurice, and other events connected with the town. These paintings are more valuable as antiquities than works of art.

There are many interesting walks and drives about Lucerne, but the Mecca for all tourists is the Lake. On the picturesque shores of this water were enacted the scenes so immortalized by Schiller in his play of "William Tell," but history and romance only serve to add to the charms of this delightful body of water. The greatest length, from Lucerne to Fluelen is twenty-seven miles, while its broadest space is three miles. Excursion boats and pleasure crafts plow its waters day and night. It would be impossible to give any idea of the vast number of attractions it affords, but I must mention the small village of Sisikon, at the mouth of the Riemstadtenthal, at the base of the Axen Mountain, where, after a few moments' ascent, you are at Tell's chapel. This chapel was erected in 1388, and has recently been restored. It is located on the spot where Tell escaped from the boat of Gessler, the Austrian governor, by springing ashore. This was originally dedicated in the presence of 114 persons who had been personally acquainted with Tell. Each year a service is held here,

The Jungfrau from Interlaken.

on the Friday after Ascension Day, in commemoration of the national hero, and is attended by the peasantry of the forest cantons, who come in boats gaily decorated.

A stay of three days at Lucerne is only an aggravation to the average tourist. A month would pass much quicker than a week in the average resort.

While at Lucerne we took the steamer for Vitznau, where we ascended the Rigi-Kulm, by railway. The summit was reached in a little less than an hour and a half and here on this mountain top, 5900 feet high, we had a panoramic view of mountains, lakes and rivers, as far as the eye could reach. Opposite us was the Pilatus Mountain, said to be the spot where Pontius Pilate killed himself after the crucifixion. This is also reached by rail. Good hotels are to be found on all mountain summits accessible. One thing I noticed in particular, vegetation and grass to the very top. This is something we do not get on our own mountains of New Hampshire. It is a grand sight to take a field glass and have in full view a snow-clad top with the green grass peeping out in patches here and there.

The Captain was passing out of his hotel one morning, when a slightly-built, gentlemanly appearing native bowed very politely and said, "*C'est beau matin.*"

It so happened the Captain had heard this so often he had become familiar with the meaning, which is, "This is a fine morning."

Quickly turning around, the Captain returned the salutation and replied, "*Oui, Monsieur; Quo Vadis?*"

I almost gasped for breath and immediately taking the Captain by the arm and leading him away, asked him what he meant.

"Why," replied the Captain, "was not my answer correct?"

"What answer," I asked.

"Didn't he say it was a fine morning?"

I nodded assent, and the Captain continued :

"And didn't I reply plainly, ' Yes sir, where are you going?' "

At this point, I was obliged to call for something strong to build up my nerves, "*Quo Vadis*" being the Latin for "Whither Goest Thou?" but the Captain had taken it for French and had sprung it upon the native.

From Lucerne we took the mountain railway for a four hours' ride over the Brunig Pass to Interlaken. The journey was a slow one, but

The Snow-Clad Jungfrau.

interesting from the moment we started until we reached our destination. The mountain scenery, the valleys dotted with little Swiss villages were enchanting. Arriving at Brienz, we took a steamer across the Brienz Lake and in an hour found ourselves at Interlaken, ready to repair to our rooms, but eager to leave them for the dinner, which was ready for us.

There is a legend at Interlaken to the effect that when the Garden of Eden was removed from the earth by ministering angels, they hovered over the Alps with their burden, and were so enchanted at the sight of the majestic snow-clad Jungfrau and the two splendid azure mountain lakes beneath it, that they placed a part of the garden at her foot and the other part between the lakes, in order to render the beauty of the splendid landscape complete. Interlaken was formerly the abode of the monks, but after centuries they went away and left the place to the natives, who lived here alone, and the outside world knew but little of the beauty and splendor that rested beneath these mountain peaks. Wandering tourists finally visited here, and soon the name and fame of Interlaken became world wide. Here is a scene of continual fashion and gaiety during the summer season.

There is an erroneous idea that in order to reach this spot one has to be drawn over high mountains; such is not the case. I came that way to enjoy the entrancing scenery, but railroads and steamboats afford several ways in and out of the town. Interlaken is protected from the north winds by a mountain rampart 6000 to 7000 feet high, as well as against the south storms. To the stranger on his first visit here the great Jungfrau, 13,762 feet high, looms up in all its majestic splendor, with its snow-clad peaks, the Queen of the Alps, while the Harderwand, called the lord of the mountains, looks down upon you. This is one of the few with a legend. "Hardermannli" was a monk of the monastery; he loved a nun and eloped with her; pursued, he hastened to the mountain, carrying his beloved in his arms, and there they found shelter.

Interlaken has all the attractions of an inland summer resort. Pretty shops with tempting goods to offer tourists. It might be well to say just here that the great majority of these stores are operated by fakirs. Extravagant prices are often charged, therefore, if you happen to see something you would like to take away, first get the price, then make an offer—and be sure you make it low enough, and you

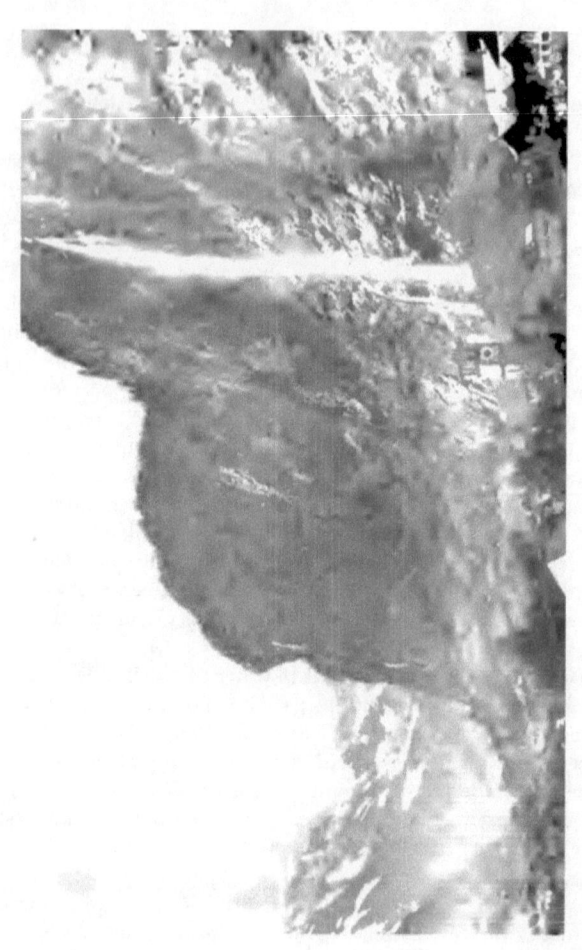

will get it. This not only applies to Interlaken but to all these Swiss cities and towns, as well as to most of the cities of the continent.

There are no public buildings here of special attractiveness. In winter, or out of season, there is a population of only 4000 people at Interlaken. The cursaal, or concert hall, is a large building where three concerts are given daily. The morning concert is from 7 to 8 o'clock, and during the selections the visitors sit at tables and drink whey. The afternoon concert is from 3 to 4, and the people drink beer. The evening concert is from 8:30 to 10:30 when the people drink wine. Here and also at Lucerne gambling is practiced on a limited or genteel scale. It is not a game of faro, but miniature racing horses or railroad trains, and as the evil must exist, the betting is small, usually one franc. Interlaken has a large number of first-class hotels, and they usually find guests enough to keep them full.

The Captain took a stroll with me visiting the stores, and at one place he had some difficulty in making the attendant understand what he wanted, so he began explaining in a very loud tone. I nudged him and asked him why he spoke so loud, as the clerk was not deaf.

"I want him to understand what I say," was the reply. But the clerk failed to understand.

While at Interlaken we took a carriage ride to Lauterbrunnen to visit the celebrated Staubbach Falls, which descend from an elevation of nearly 1000 feet almost perpendicularly, the precipitation of which causes the descending stream to first become thin as a cloud and then almost evaporate to smoke or dust-like mist in which the rays of the sun appear like a moving rainbow. On our way out we drove to Grindelwald, where we had a magnificent view of the glaciers. The trip was eventful for its delightful scenery, and as our mountain carriage rolled along, we here and there heard the sound of the alpine horn, and passed the cottages of the peasant lace-makers, who hurried out and followed our carriages in their eagerness to sell their wares. As the mountain side came in view, here and there on their lofty tops, could be seen the homes of the Swiss mountaineers, truly a reminder of those stories of Swiss life that the man of the present read during his boyhood.

As our carriages approached the mountain climb, we were met by half a dozen boys from 9 to 14 years, some with large bunches of freshly cut leaves, or others with large foxtails, and as the horses be-

Brunig Pass and Railway.

gan to climb, they began to brush them vigorously to keep off the flies, although the day we took our journey, hardly a fly was to be seen. Yet in spite of our protest, the boys kept up the brushing and followed us for nearly an hour, and when we reached the mountain top, they passed their hats around for "some centimes."

On our return, when about half an hour's ride from Interlaken, we came across a herd of goats, possibly 150, which were in a pasture, and were being gathered together to be driven home. It appeared to us afterward that this herd belonged in Interlaken, and were gathered by two or three persons, who passed through the streets early every morning blowing a sort of whistle, and as they passed along, the goats would come out of their homes and follow. In the evening they are returned for the milking.

The night before our departure from Interlaken, while the Captain and myself were enjoying our dinner, a gentleman who sat just beyond him endeavored to attract his attention, and when he had done so, remarked:

"*Donez-moi le menu, s'il vous plait, monsieur?*"

The Captain looked at him for a moment in surprise, and then, turning to me, asked what that rooster wanted.

I informed the Captain that he had asked him to "Please pass the menu."

"And what," asked the Captain, "is the menu?"

When I passed it over to him, the Captain gave me a look of scorn, as he replied, "Why didn't you say the gentleman wanted the program?" And as we passed out I was undecided whether to continue the journey through Switzerland or hie myself to some convent in that location.

CHAPTER X.

Adieu to the Land of the Swiss.

AFTER leaving Interlaken we next stopped at Berne, one of the oldest, if not the oldest, cities in Switzerland. Berne is the capital, yet it is antique, antique from the word go.

Its main business thoroughfare is a street devoted to market purposes, while the stores are on an elevated sidewalk arched in and covered over as the buildings project out even to the gutter line.

The Captain wanted a necktie. He could not be induced to take anything but a four-in-hand. In one store we entered, the attendant could not speak English, so one of our party undertook to do the conversation in German, but at this the Captain protested.

"What is the matter," I asked, "why not make your purchase through this party?"

"Because," replied the Captain, "I do not propose to get buncoed; let him talk English."

Well, we finally got the tie.

Berne has a population of between 45,000 and 50,000 people. It derived its name from Berne, or Bear, and the attraction of the city is the bear pit opened up on a public thoroughfare, and the moment a stranger sets foot in town he is either taken or starts for the Bears. In fact, everything there is bear. The noted Zeitglocken Tower and Bear Chimes always attract a crowd in front of it at 12 o'clock each day, when it peals forth, and the bears march round three or four times, while the clown strikes the bell. This is an automaton in the tower.

There are a number of interesting places in the city, such as several churches, the Federal Council Hall or House of Parliament, a very plain and unpretentious structure. There is an historical museum, an old town hall, a picture gallery, university, military academy, statues, fountains and other attractions. Two days will be sufficient for any one to see all that Berne contains, and after a visit to such places as Zurich, Lucerne, Interlaken etc., the place seems anything but attractive. There is a nice suburb and beautiful parks.

From Berne we had an interesting ride to Territet-Glion, another Swiss paradise, situated at the foot of the Alps and on the shore of that majestic Swiss lake, Geneva, called here Lake Leman. This body of water is 58 miles long, and, like Lake Lucerne, goes under a different name in many sections. Territet is located in the heart of the best grape and wine making section of Switzerland. The hotels here are the finest in the country and, strange to say in this mountain region, this is a winter resort, the season commencing September 1, and continuing to June 1, with a little falling off in December and January, while June, July and August are the dullest months of the year. The grape cure is the attraction, next to the magnificent situation. In fact, this is called the Swiss Riviera.

Close by, and within sight from the water's edge, lie the towns of Montreaux, Vevey and Savoy. Boats ply the lake and excursions are numerous. The mountain view is superb, in fact, the town lies at the very foot of one of these hills, which rises in all its grandeur and forms a background. I think I am nearly right when I say that the whole actual width of the town below the mountains sides is not over 400 feet. Toward the south the eye can glance from summit to summit of the lofty peaks, resting now on a group of rocks standing out boldly against the horizon, now on the wooded slopes forming the pedestal of the mountain-chain which runs from Savoy to the Alps of Valais. The seven pointed diadem and its silvery mantle, the Dent-du-Midi, dominates the landscape and fascinates the gaze by the unsullied purity of its eternal snows and the majestic grandeur of its outlines. At its feet the river Rhone pursues its tranquil course through the plain, ere it flows into the lake. In the west, far beyond the shining surface of the lake, is to be seen the gentle outline of the Jura, which separates two republics. In the east, at the foot of the steep slope, clothed in chestnut trees, stands in all its solitary glory, the ancient castle of Chillon, the famous prison house of Bonnivard. On the north are to be seen the vast acres of grape vines as they are terraced on steep slopes, some places mountain sides.

This is the picture of Territet-Glion. And yet this little town of possibly 2000 or less people, has a double track railroad running through it, an electric car line, a cable railway to the mountain summit and steamboat lines.

General View of Berne.

But there is the old Castle of Chillon, made famous in early days by the deviltry enacted within its walls, and famous in later days by Lord Byron, in his beautiful tribute to it. The history of the Castle of Chillon dates back to the middle ages. During the first years of the eighteenth century, Count Thomas I. of Savoy, famous for his chivalrous character, thought of converting the castle into a residence for himself, and did something in that direction and several changes were made. At the beginning of the present century, it became the property of the canton. At the time I visited it workmen were engaged in restoring it and it is proposed to make a national museum out of it, when ready.

> "Lake Leman lies by Chillon's walls,
> A thousand feet in depth below,
> Its massy waters meet and flow,
> Thus much the fathom-line was sent
> From Chillon's snow-white battlement,
> Which round about the wave inthralls."

Thus wrote Byron in his "Prisoner of Chillon."

In its early years the castle controlled this part of the country. Directly opposite it rises a mountain and only one road passes between the castle and the mountain, while the other side of the castle is bounded by the lake. The old order of things was enforced, those who pass must pay tribute. In 1536 when the cantons Vaud and Geneva obtained their independence, the Castle of Chillon resisted for a long time, but it was eventually captured by the Bernese, aided by a flotilla from Geneva. Bonnivard and the other captives obtained their liberty. Bonnivard was prior of St. Victor and endeavored to free the Genoese from the tyranny of Charles V. of Savoy, so that he became very obnoxious to that monach, who had him seized and confined in the castle, where he lay for six years in a dungeon. The pillar to which he was chained and the ring to which he was fastened still stands, while the floor around it is much worn. Byron beautifully describes the effect of his imprisonment in his "Prisoner of Chillon."

> "It might be months, or years or days—
> I kept no count, I took no note—
> I had no hope my eyes to raise,
> And clear them of their dreary mote;
> At last men came to set me free,
> I asked not why, I recked not where,
> It was at length the same to me,
> Fettered or fetterless to be,
> I learned to love despair.

The Bear Pit at Berne.

> And thus when they appeared at last,
> And all my bonds aside were cast,
> These heavy walls to me had grown
> A hermitage and all mine own,
> And half I felt as they were come
> To tear me from a second home.
> With spiders I had friendship made
> And watched them in their sullen trade,
> Had seen the mice by moonlight play,
> And why should I feel less than they?
> We were all inmates of one place,
> And I, the monarch of each race,
> Had power to kill, yet strange to tell,
> In quiet we had learned to dwell.
> My very chains and I grew friends,
> So much a long communion tends
> To make us what we are; even I
> Regained my freedom with a sigh."

It seems that Byron was ignorant of the history of Bonnivard when he wrote the "Prisoner of Chillon." Bonnivard had no brother and none died in the castle. The real Bonnivard was a wealthy young man, son of the Lord of Lorne, and he inherited the rich priory of St. Victor from his uncle when he was only sixteen years old. This property lying close to Geneva he espoused that city's quarrel with the Duke of Savoy and was confined in prison for two years. After his release from imprisonment he again took up arms to recover his lost possessions and, with the aid of Geneva, did so, and afterward entered the service of that city. It was after this that he was again captured and imprisoned for six years in the Castle of Chillon. He died at the advanced age of seventy-five years.

The Castle of Chillon dates from the ninth century. In 830 Louis le Debonnaire imprisoned the Abbe Wala, who had instigated his sons to rebellion, in a castle in this section that answers the description of this place. Over the castellan's entrance are the following words inscribed there by the Bernese in 1643: "Gott der Herr segne den Einund Ansgang," which translated reads, "God bless all who come in and go out."

On the pillars of the prison and floor of the castles are to be seen the names of many noted men cut in this soft stone by themselves during visits here. I was surprised at the distinctness of some. First there was Lord Byron's, then Eugene Sue, Victor Hugo, George Sand, Shelley and Dumas.

I called the attention of the Captain to these names, and told him they were done by the hands of these famous men. He looked on

for a moment and then, drawing his penknife, astonished me by starting in to cut on a smooth place on the pillar.

"What are you doing?" I asked.

"Going to carve my name," was the reply.

When I told him it was against the rules and punishable by a fine, he asked how much.

"Ten francs," I answered.

"Ten francs," he replied, "why, that is only two dollars. It is the cheapest advertisement the Emerson Shoe ever had."

But by a determined effort I got him away.

From Territet-Glion, a pleasant ride of about one and one half hours by rail brought us to our next stopping place, Martigny, where we caught a glimpse of many old monasteries, some built five, some six, and some seven hundred years ago. Martigny is the starting place for Chamounix and Mont Blanc. The trip is made by diligences over the Tete-Noire pass, and takes about ten hours. Leaving Martigny at 7:30 A. M., the road leads in a zigzag direction to an elevation of nearly four thousand feet. In fact, it is a ride across the Alps.

It was while we were enjoying the grand scenery in all directions that I asked the Captain if he realized we were crossing the Alps—the same Alps crossed by the great Napoleon and made a part of his famous history. The Captain did not enthuse much; he quietly drew from his vest pocket the only remaining cigar he managed to land on that side of the water and, after lighting it, remarked, "Well, suppose Napoleon did cross here. That was years and years ago, but today, I am crossing."

I leaned back in my carriage and could hardly decide whether I would quietly drop off the mountain side or proceed on the journey.

With a two-hour rest on the mountain summit, we proceeded and arrived at Chamounix at 5:30 P. M., with the snow-clad top of Mont Blanc looming up in the rear of our hotel and the Glacier des Bossons in full view. It was a gorgeous sunset, and an equally gorgeous sunrise the following morning, and the sight presented was one I will never forget. At 9 o'clock the morning after our arrival we straddled mules and wended our way to the glacier and up the side of Mont Blanc. The journey was one long to be remembered. I am glad I made the trip, but I would not do it again for many a hundred dol-

lar bill. We were landed directly on the glacier, and made a tour of the ice grotto constructed beneath it.

Before starting I asked the Captain if he intended to go up on a mule. He replied that such was his intention, but I doubt if he would do it again if he was assured a good and true deed of the whole of Switzerland. The mule that was selected for the Captain drew a line on the flies, and insisted on occasional gymnastics that made the Captain wish he was back at his hotel in safety.

It is an old saying, "See Naples and die," but I believe this was a mistake. It should have been, "See the Alps! Away to the moutains, and live long." Chamounix is a small mountain village lying at the foot of Mont Blanc and is the shrine sought by all pilgrims to this grand mountain. It lies in France and near the Switzerland frontier, yet Chamounix is always associated with Switzerland and the Alps scenery in guide books. Of course, Mont Blanc is the chief attraction, while the scenery in all directions is superb.

Just here I might say that the first to ascend this mountain were Jacques Balmat and Dr. Paccard, who climbed to the top on the 8th of August, 1786. There is a little history in connection with these two men. Balmat was born January 19, 1762, in the hamlet of Pelorins in the vicinity of the glacier of the same name. His house is still standing. He was only twenty four years old, and the father of a family, when De Saussure offered a reward for the discovery of a route to the summit of Mont Blanc. Balmat, who had a love for the mountains, determined to find the route. He tried several ways across the Glacier des Bois and failed, then across the Glacier des Bossons and spent a night there in the snow, but was obliged to return the next day on account of a fog. Then he ventured by the Rochers Rouges, and climbed still higher, but was obliged to return a part of the way, where he spent the night on the icy mountain, but the next morning was clear and beautiful, and he felt sure he had discovered the route, and immediately returned to Dr. Paccard and communicated to him the news.

So, on Monday, August 7, these two men left Chamounix, and the following day at two o'clock in the afternoon they reached the right shoulder of Mont Blanc, the extreme point obtained by Balmat in his former venture. Dr. Paccard was exhausted, and declined to proceed further, so Balmat started on alone, until he found he had reached

the summit. The victory was won. Mont Blanc was conquered. Balmat returned to his companion and, after rousing him, chafed his numb limbs and induced him to start on the way, and at six o'clock in the evening the top was reached. A market woman at Chamounix saw two little specks and spread the news, and the villagers turned out to witness the scene. Balmat and Paccard remained thirty-five minutes on the summit, and then started downward. At eleven o'clock they regained their former camping place where they remained over night and the next morning descended to Chamounix, where they were met and feted by the people. Balmat received a present and diploma from the King of Sardinia, and a subscription was opened for him, and on August 13 he visited De Saussure, who received him with joy, and gave him the promised reward. In 1787 Horace De Saussure made the ascent. So much for the discovery. Since then the mountain has been scaled by many; many lives have been lost, among them two Americans, John Randall, father of John C. Randall of John H. Pray & Sons Co., Boston, and Dr. Bean.

Leaving Chamounix by diligence we journeyed to Cluses where we took the train to Geneva. The trip is made in about six hours. It was while we were making this journey that we floated our American flags and were met by a party of Frenchmen who eyed the Captain as he waved his umbrella with flag attached, and we could hear their only remark. It was "Yankee Doodles," and as they passed the Captain arose in his seat and waved his flag and shouted back, "Yes, we're Yankee Doodles, and don't you forget it." A few miles further on, as we were making a sharp wind around a mountain side, we noticed a carriage coming in the opposite direction, and as it approached we discerned that it contained four or five ladies and gentlemen. "Out with your flags," shouted the Captain, and out they came, and no sooner did the approaching party see "Old Glory" than they stood up and shouted, "Three cheers for Uncle Sam." We had encountered a party of our own country people on our way from Mont Blanc.

While not the largest city in Switzerland, Geneva is the gayest, and like Zurich and Lucerne, is a beautiful resort during the season. It has a population of about 80,000 people, and is grandly located on the lake bearing its name.

I was strolling along the Quai, the main business street, with the Captain, and we chanced to enter a store where the attendant spoke

The Captain and His Mule.

very little English. Suddenly the Captain asked him if he would be so kind as to tell him under what name they called their money in Italy.

"Liras," was the answer.

"Come out of here," said the Captain, grabbing me by the arm, and as I glanced at him I saw his face was a deep red.

"What is the matter?" I asked.

"That chump called us liars, it's either get out quick or I lick him," replied the Captain. In order to have peace and harmony, I got out.

Geneva is distinctly French, not only in its manners and customs, but its language. Yet it is cosmopolitan, and has a society to render the sojourn of American and English tourists pleasant. There are a number of attractive monuments and fountains, and bridges span the course that runs from the lake in swift currents and is utilized for its power. It is a wonderful waterway. Here is the Hotel de Ville or Town Hall, where the Arbitration Court on the Alabama claims sat in 1872. The St. Peters Cathedral, Protestant, built in 1024 in the Romanesque style, where Calvin once preached, and containing his chair, which is in a good state of preservation. By the way, this was Calvin's stronghold. He came here in 1536 and died here in 1564, and was buried in the cemetery of Plainpalais. There are several other interesting churches and public buildings, including an University with old manuscripts, many of Calvin's. A fine palm garden and parks lend attraction to the visitor.

During the evenings, in the summer seasons, the sidewalks in front of cafés are crowded, and bands and orchestras play from 8:30 to 11 o'clock. Sunday is no exception for these occasions. Geneva, like all other places, has its wickedness with its goodness.

The morning of our departure the Captain hailed me in the hotel corridor, and asked me where our next destination was.

"To Paris," I replied, "We go to Paris today."

"Three cheers for Paris!" shouted the Captain.

"What are you cheering for?" I asked.

"Wait until we get there and I will let you know," was the only response I could get from him.

And the train started, bearing two Yankees, for Paris.

CHAPTER XI.

How to Do Paris.

"DO YOU see those bright lights in the distance?" I asked the Captain, as we were speeding along in the cars, late at night.

"Yes," was his reply, as he gazed out of the window in the direction indicated.

"That is Paris," I answered.

The Captain immediately got up and took off his traveling cap, packed it in his grip, dusted his coat and put on his hat. He was in a nervous state.

In ten minutes we rolled into the station and alighted from the train. Our baggage was passed, and I hailed a cab to convey us to our hotel. The moment the Captain took his seat, he shouted:

"Say, driver!"

I stopped him short and told him the man did not know what he said, that he must address him as *cocher*.

"*Cocher*," called the Captain.

"*Oui, monsieur*," was the reply.

"How long will it take you to drive us to the *Moulin Rouge?*" shouted the Captain.

I nearly fainted.

It was with some difficulty I gave my companion to understand that the hour was late and we had come a long distance and must go to our hotel and rest, but after a bit of diplomacy on my part the Captain succumbed and we were soon settled in our hotel.

"You wanted to know why I gave three cheers for Paris when we started," he said, as we were taking a light lunch. "Well, it was the prospects of a view of the *Moulin Rouge*, and you have spoiled the whole show."

I admitted my supposed error, but as we had over two weeks in the gay metropolis, I told him he would have ample opportunity to see Paris as she was.

I am not going to attempt to give any historical data about Paris. If I did this chapter would be continued until the end of the book. With a population of over 2,500,000, Paris was the second largest city in the world, but that distinction now goes to Greater New York who will give London such a tussle for first place that it will be a hotter contest than an American league game of baseball.

The grand system of boulevards that cross the city are the finest in the world, and neither New York or any other American city will ever be able to compete with Paris in this direction. The beauty of the avenues lies in their distance and straightness; both sides are lined with trees and they are paved with either wood or asphalt, are always clean, and carriages driving over them make but little noise. At night the streets are finely lighted with both gas and electricity— in fact, Paris is the best lighted city in the world. Standing in the Place de la Opera of an evening and viewing the Boulevard des Italiens, Avenue de la Opera, Rue de la Paix and the Boulevard des Capucines, a sight is presented equal to that of fairyland.

Paris is, or rather was, full of Americans while I was there, during the month of August. They thronged the streets, filled the stores and were to be found in all the public places. I do not know what Paris shopkeepers would do if the American exodus ceased.

The average tourist who first visits Paris, naturally wants to see the most interesting places at a glance, therefore I will describe, as briefly as possible, such that could be seen in a stay of from one to two weeks.

First, let us take the churches. Of course everybody has heard of the Notre Dame and the Madeleine. They are two of the most noted churches in the world. The Notre Dame is the cathedral of the Archbishopric of Paris, and was founded in 1163 on the very site of a church built in the fourth century. The front is surmounted by two square towers and the carvings in the right portal represent the Last Judgment, while the relief on the left portal represents the Burial of the Virgin. Immediately above these portals is the Galerie des Rois, a series of niches containing statues of twenty-eight French kings. The church contains some fine ancient stained glass windows well worth inspection. The house will hold 20,000 persons. The choir or burial chapel which surrounds the main altar contains monuments to noted archbishops of Paris, who had been famous in their day.

The wood carvings are especially worth examining. In the treasury is to be found a vast collection of solid gold and silver ornaments, used on altars, and many set in precious stones of priceless value. These have been collected for ages, and were presents from kings and queens. Here is also to be seen what is supposed to be fragments of the crown of thorns and the true cross as well as a nail from the latter, also many ecclesiastical vestments embroidered in gold and silver and set with precious stones. Large silver busts of St. Denis and St. Louis are shown, as well as the blood-stained garments of Archbishop Darboy, who was murdered by the Commune. During the first revolution the Notre Dame was condemned to destruction, but the decree was rescinded, the sculptures only being demolished. It was at this time converted into a "Temple of Reason," but Napoleon I. restored it to its original purpose in 1802. In the Commune of 1871 it was used as a military depot and afterwards an attempt was made to burn it, but fortunately without success.

In leaving the church I noticed two contribution boxes posted in one of the aisles. The first was labeled "For Souls in Purgatory," while the other bore a card "For the tooth of St. Peter." The Captain insisted in dropping ten centimes in each box.

The Madeleine, or Church of St. Mary Magdalene, was started in 1764 and the ceremonies of laying the foundation were by Louis XV. The building was not completed until 1842, or 78 years after it was commenced. This was caused by the interruptions made by wars and changes of government during that period. The cost of the building was $2,600,000. The structure is a most imposing one, and the front is supported by great columns. Over the front the carvings represent the Last Judgment, while the two bronze doors are adorned with groups illustrating the Ten Commandments. There are no stained glass nor side windows in the Madeleine, it is a church without windows, but, in place, six niches are built on each side, containing life size statues of the saints. The music here is very fine, especially Sunday morning. During the civil war which followed the siege of Paris, the Madeleine was in considerable danger. A barricade defended by cannon was erected by the insurgents across the Rue Royale, immediately in front of the church, and in the conflict between the troops of the Republic and the Commune, many houses were destroyed. When the rebels were finally overcome, hundreds sought refuge in the Madeleine and were killed on the spot.

Notre Dame, Paris.

The morning after our arrival in Paris, I came down to the reading room of our hotel, and found the Captain busily looking over the contents of a French morning paper and humming in rather a loud tone, "The Watch on the Rhine," while near by sat half a dozen angry looking Frenchmen, who nervously glanced at their papers and then at the Captain. I immediately took in the situation, and going up to my friend quietly asked him what he was doing, and if he did not notice that he was attracting attention.

"What's the matter with me?" asked the Captain.

"Why, that tune you are humming," I replied.

"Well, what of it?" came the question.

"It is the 'Watch on the Rhine,' the German national tune, and those people do not like it," I replied. "Don't you know there is a hatred between the French and Germans?"

"Was that the 'Watch on the Rhine?'" asked the Captain, "why I thought it was 'The Marseilles,' and I was simply humming it to please these people."

I asked the Captain out to have a cigar, in order to get him away.

A drive, the most beautiful drive in the world, is to be found over the Champs Elysees and through the Bois de Boulogne. The Champs Elysees starts in at the Place de la Concorde, the largest and finest square in Paris. Yes, the same may be said of this as of the above thoroughfare, the finest square in the world. The Place de la Concorde is 1200 by 700 feet, and at night presents a dazzling sight.

Here also is erected the Obelisk of Luxor, and this site has a tragic history. It was during the Reign of Terror, in 1793, that a guillotine was erected on this spot, and its first victims were Louis XVI. and Marie Antoinette. Between January of that year and May 1795, upward of 2000 persons were beheaded here.

From the center of this place the Champs Elysees leads to the Arc de Triomphe, a magnificent avenue lined with elegant residences including the Palais de l'Elysees, erected in 1718, and now the official residence of the President of the Republic. The avenue is lined on both sides with trees and promenades. The Arc de Triomphe is the largest triumphal arch in existence. It was begun by Napoleon I. in 1806, and completed in 1836 by Louis Philippe. The arch is 67 feet high and 46 feet wide, while the whole structure is 160 feet high and 146 feet wide and 72 feet deep. It cost upward of $2,000,000.

Champs Elysees, Paris.

From the arc lead twelve beautiful avenues, the chief of which is the Bois de Boulogne. This section of the city is a wooded one, and covers hundreds of acres, with roads and paths innumerable.

On the other side of the Seine, in the rear of the Notre Dame, is the morgue, open for inspection daily. Here are displayed on marble slabs the dead bodies of those found in the river and other places, who are not known. These slabs are placed in front of a glass partition, where the public can view the dead, and if possible recognize who they are. The clothes in which they are found are displayed with them. By a system of refrigeration it is said that these bodies can be kept for three months.

The Jardin des Plantes, or Palm Garden, lies a little distance beyond the morgue. Here is a good zoological show, but a poor plant display, when some of the other gardens I have visited are considered.

Near the foot of the Rue de la Paix, which starts in next to the Avenue de la Opera, opposite the Opera House, is the Place Vendome, where stands the Column Vendome, erected in 1806 by Napoleon I. to commemorate his victories over the Russians and Austrians. The column is of masonry encrusted with bronze plates, and is 142 feet high and 13 feet in diameter.

While located at our hotel in Paris, the Captain noticed a very handsome clock in the reading room and inquired of the manager where it came from.

" Right here in Paris," was the reply. " I bought it in this city."

Nothing further was said until a few days after, when the Captain again accosted the manager and remarked to him that he understood him to say the clock in question was bought in Paris.

" So it was," he replied.

" Well, that is very strange," remarked the Captain, " for I have looked your directory over to find the fellow who made it, but his name does not appear."

" I do not understand how you could have looked for his name," was the reply, " when I did not tell you what it was."

" His name," said the Captain, "can't I read ? " There it is right on the face of the clock, ' *Tempus Fugit, Paris, France.*' "

And as I was just approaching the Captain and heard the conversation, I made a bee line for the smoking room.

A place that will undoubtedly interest an American tourist in Paris is the Catacombs. Admission can usually be obtained by application to the Prefect of the Seine, at the Hotel de Ville or city hall. I had no difficulty in securing a permit. The Catacombs are open for the inspection of ticket holders the first and third Saturdays of each month. This burial place, or rather resting place for the bones of the departed, is located on the left bank of the river, and covers an area almost the length of the city. It has about sixty entrances. Formerly this was a subterranean quarry, and was worked as far back as the Roman period. Upon entering the Catacombs each visitor must carry a torch, which costs 50 centimes (10 cents) at the entrance, and included in this is a guard of cardboard to protect the clothing from the melting wax. It takes about one hour to make the tour. The quarries were first used for Catacombs in 1786, and during the French Revolution and Reign of Terror immense numbers of bodies and bones were thrown in these cavities in a confused state, and remained so until 1810 when a regular system was organized for the arrangement and disposition of their resting places.

Of course every one going to Paris wants to visit and ascend the Eiffel Tower, which was the attraction of the last Paris exposition, and was what suggested our World's Fair Ferris Wheel. The Eiffel Tower is located on a portion of the 1889 exhibition ground, close by the Seine and opposite the Trocadero. This enormous structure is the loftiest monument in the world, being 984 feet high, or nearly twice as high as the Washington monument at our national capital, which is 555 feet. It is indeed an interesting specimen of what can be accomplished in accurate skill in design and modern engineering. Owing to an optical delusion the tower appears at close range much lower than it really is. The foundation was sunk forty-six feet, and the base of the structure covers two and one-half acres, consisting of a graceful framework of iron. The tower has three landing places or platforms. The first is 190 feet high, and has an area of 5860 square yards. The second is 380 feet high, and covers an area of 32 square yards, while the third is 904 feet high, and will hold 800 people at one time. On a clear day there is a view of ninety miles in length. An elevator makes the trips up and down at a cost of twenty cents for first platform, forty cents for second and eighty cents for third platform. On Sundays and fete days the price is just one-half.

The Trocadero and Bridge, Paris.

Restaurants, cafés, stores and a theatre are to be seen on the different landings.

The Captain was in the smoking room of our hotel one evening, when I introduced him to a gentleman with whom I was conversing, and whom I had met on several occasions while in Paris.

"I am glad to meet you, Captain," was the response, "I have observed you several times, and supposed you were an English visitor here."

"What's that?" said the Captain.

"I took you for an Englishman," was the reply.

"Well, sir," replied the Captain, "I am not an Englishman. I am an American, sir—an American; you might call me a Yankee."

The party in question afterward referred to the Captain as a "real live Yankee."

By the way, the American tourist will find some queer things to understand on his first visit to Paris. Let us take for example the theatre or opera. If you secure your seats in advance, that is, as late as 5 P. M. the day of the performance, and even go to the box office to buy them, there is an extra charge of two francs (forty cents) each, and when your ticket is handed you, you pay ten centimes (two cents) for stamping it. In the ordinary theatre a reserved seat is not a reserved seat. By this I mean you do not know what you are going to have until you arrive at the house, when you pass to the center corridor, where behind a long desk-like enclosure, sit three or four typical Frenchmen; sometimes they are without hats and at other times they wear tall silk head coverings. Your tickets are passed over to them, and they return you others, which practically give you your seats. If you have more than one they are liable to be separated. If a certain row contains twenty-four seats, twenty-four unnumbered tickets are sold, and as the audience pass in, the numbers are given them, so that first comers usually fare the best.

Passing in, you are met by old women ushers. When I say old women, I mean it in every sense, as their ages seem to be from forty-five to sixty-five with a number who looked as if they might be seventy-five, and they were homely dames at that. It seems to me that good-looking young women might be desirable in this position, but why the Parisians inflict those old crones on their audiences is more than I can understand.

If you want a program, you must pay for it, and in one instance the usher forced a little stool under my feet, much against my wishes, and then demanded pay for it. Before the curtain rises, instead of the usual ring of the bell, there is a series of hard knocks behind the curtain, that might be done by a mallet. This is followed by three, two and one knocks, when the curtain rises. At the Chatelet Theatre, where spectacular shows are given, "Michel Strogroff" was the attraction. Here, at intermission, men wearing long aprons, like shop hands, passed through the audience selling oranges. Imagine an American theatre audience eating oranges between the acts, and this in August!

One noon arriving at my hotel a little late for lunch, I observed the Captain was in rather a nervous condition, and he asked me if I would be kind enough to make my stay in the dining room as short as possible, as he wanted to see me; therefore, taking a quick lunch, I returned to the Captain, and he asked me if I would like to take a carriage and go out to see "*Complet.*"

"Go out where?" I asked.

"*Complet,*" was the reply, "I have been trying to get there for the last ten days. There are cars and buses that go out there, but each time I have endeavored to board one the driver or conductor has informed me that he had all the passengers the law would allow; therefore, I have not been able to get out to the place, and as I observe the name on so many cars and buses, it must be an interesting place to visit."

When I informed the Captain the word "*Complet*" on a car or bus meant that it was full, and no more passengers would be allowed, he grew red in the face and actually accused me of trying to evade the visit with him, and the last I saw of him, he was endeavoring to make a hack driver understand he wanted to go to "*Complet.*"

CHAPTER XII.

Still Doing Paris.

BY WAY of explanation, I will say that it is the custom in Paris to welcome you with a "good-day" and leave you with a "good-by" in the stores you visit. The Captain noticed this, and one day asked me if I knew the French for "good-by." I told him it was *au revoir*, and gave it no further thought until we were leaving a store where we had been making some slight purchases, when I was amazed by the Captain lifting his hat as we departed, and saying, "*Mon Dieu, Monsieur.*"

"What did you say that for?" I asked.

"I bade him good-by," replied the Captain.

"Do you know what you said to him?" I again asked.

"Yes, good-by," was the response.

"No, your remark was far different," I returned. "You said, '*Mon Dieu*,' that is French for 'My God.'"

The Captain said he would take his French lessons in the future from some one who understood the language, and not from me.

There is one thing that attracted my attention and that is the unmannerly way in which Europeans gaze at an American, particularly in hotels, and more especially in the dining rooms. I do not think this practice is as noticeable in Paris as it is in Germany and Switzerland. I have seen the natives, while at table, lean on their elbows and gaze for fully five minutes at a particular person. We would call this anything but polite, but to cap the climax is to observe them pick their teeth while so engaged, and use their knives to convey food to their mouths.

Paris has two fine art galleries, the Louvre and the Luxembourg. The Louvre is without doubt one of the most famous in the world. The foundation was laid in 1541, but this building was not wholly completed until 1852, under Napoleon III. It formed a part of the

Garden of the Tuileries, Paris.

Palace of the Tuileries. The lower floor is given up to sculptures, both ancient and modern, and contains many statues of celebrity, including, I might add, the Venus of Milo, which was found by a peasant in the island of Melos, now Milo, in 1820, and sold to the French government for 6000 francs or $1200. Several museums of an interesting character are distributed in different salons, and contain many ancient and valuable curiosities. The picture galleries contain about 3000 select works, and are distributed in about twenty-five salons. Here are to be found masterpieces of Rubens, Rembrandt, Van Dyck, and many other notable masters. It would be impossible to do them justice in a description in these pages.

The Luxembourg collection is displayed in the old Luxembourg Palace, which was erected by Marie de Medicis, widow of Henry IV., in 1615, and is now the seat of the French Senate. This palace continued to be a royal residence down to the Revolution, and its last occupant, the Count of Provence, afterwards Louis XVIII., left it in June, 1791. Part of this palace is open for inspection, except on Sundays, and will well repay a visit. The gallery, which occupies a ground floor, is in the rear of the palace, and contains only works of living artists. The collection is not very large, yet it is an interesting one and is of a less religious character than many of the collections shown in the old galleries, and is quite a relief from the regular exhibits one sees in all parts of Europe.

The most beautiful open spot in all Paris is the Garden of the Tuileries, famous the world over for its connection with the Palace of the Tuileries, the adored home of kings and emperors. Part of the garden is fenced in, and only open at certain hours. Here are to be found a large number of marble statues and groups, mostly the works of modern sculptors. A military band gives concerts in the gardens daily, with the exceptions of Mondays and Fridays, from 5 to 6 P. M.

On the left bank of the Seine, and occupying about thirty acres of ground, stands the Hotel des Invalides, or what we might call the soldiers' home. This was founded in 1670 by Louis XIV. Soldiers who have been disabled by wounds or who have given thirty years to the service of their country, are admitted here. The building was originally intended to accommodate about 5000 persons, but the average number of dwellers here is not over 400, as most of the old veterans prefer to take their pensions and live independently. The front of the building faces a large enclosure, fenced around, and in which is quite a display of cannon. Entering the building through an arched doorway one finds himself in the Cour d' Honneur, enclosed by arcades under the main building, and adorned by a series of massive paintings on the sides of the building, mostly representing scenes in the lives of Charlemagne, St. Louis, Louis XIV. and Napoleon I. In the building are to be found several military museums, open on certain days.

Passing though the arcade on the left as you enter, and through a passageway, the tourist is brought before one of the most interesting places in all France—the tomb of Napoleon I. The interior of the building is circular and finished in white marble with a magnificent dome surmounting it. The tomb is situated directly beneath the dome in an open circular crypt, twenty feet in depth and thirty-six feet in diameter. The walls are of polished granite adorned with ten marble reliefs, and there are twelve colossal statues of Victories, while six trophies, consisting of sixty battle flags gives enchantment to the last resting place of this great soldier. As I leaned over the marble balustrade, the eloquent words of Col. Robert G. Ingersoll in his "At the Tomb of Napoleon," passed through my mind. Entering this building at the right is the tomb of Joseph Bonaparte, once King of Spain, and at the left is that of Jerome Bonaparte, once King of Westphalia. In the rear is a chapel, not opened to the public, where services are held on the anniversary of his death. Opposite the entrance to the chapel, from the tomb building is the entrance to the tomb, which is twenty feet below the audience balustrade, and over the door of this entrance are these words: "*Je desire que mes cendres reposent sur les bords de la Seine, au milieu de ce peuple Francaise que j'ai tant aime*," which translated reads, "I desire that my ashes may rest on the banks of the Seine, in the midst of the French people, whom I have so well loved."

The Captain was very much impressed with this place, and while busily engaged in doing the grounds noticed several gentlemen wearing a red ribbon in their left buttonholes.

"Do you know what that signifies?" he asked.

"I told him they were members of the Legion of Honor, and thought nothing more of the matter until a day or two after, when we were on our way down the Boulevard des Italiens, and the Captain stopped before a jewelry store, in which was displayed a variety of decorations.

"I see something I have been looking for," said the Captain, as he entered the store and I followed.

When the attendant appeared the Captain pointed to a cross of the Legion of Honor, and asked the price.

"Fifty francs," was the reply.

"I'll take it," said the Captain as he deposited that amount on the counter.

"What did you buy that for?" I asked, as we left the store.

"It's the Legion of Honor," he replied.

"But what are you going to do with it?" I again asked.

"Wear it," said the Captain.

"But in order to wear it you must be decorated for some valiant deed, and this is done by the President of France," I replied.

"That's all right as far as you have got it," was the reply, "but I have carried my gun and swung my sword on many a bloody battle-field in the war for the Union, and I propose to decorate myself."

And then the Captain lit a cigar that cost him one franc fifty centimes, while I walked by his side a much meeker man than was Moses himself.

The Palais Royal—it does not look much like a palace in these last days of the nineteenth century—is said to be an accurate reflex of the history of Paris for two and a half centuries. This historic building was erected by Cardinal Richelieu in 1629, and was originally called the Palais Cardinal. Anne of Austria, with her two sons, Louis XIV. and Philip of Orleans, occupied it after the cardinal's death. Since her day it has been known by its present name. On ascending the throne Louis XIV. presented the palace to his younger brother, and after Philip's death two generations of the Orleans family occupied it as a residence; through them it was brought in bad repute. Having exhausted his means the grandson of Philip built a series of arcades or stores around the courtyard, and let them to shopkeepers. They are occupied for that purpose to this day, and a journey around among these stores must be nearly one mile in length. I toured this section. It is indeed interesting, as fully one-half of the stores are for the sale of jewelry, from the bogus to the finest made goods.

Under the consulate of Napoleon I. the palace was called the galité, and later Palais du Tribunat, but at the restoration the

Tomb of Napoleon, Hotel des Invalides, Paris.

palace again reverted to the Orleans family, and Louis Philippe occupied it until 1830. In the revolution of 1848 the mob wrecked the royal apartments and destroyed the greater part of the pictures. From then until the time of Napoleon III. the palace was called Palais National, but when he became emperor, Napoleon restored its present name. In 1871 the Communists repeated the raid of 1848 on the royal apartments, but luckily most of the works of value had been removed. The south wing was destroyed by fire, but has since been restored.

On the highest ground in Paris, on the left bank of the Seine, is a most imposing structure built in the form of a Greek cross, known as the Pantheon. The foundation was laid in 1764 by Louis XV. It is 375 feet long by 275 feet wide, with a dome 272 feet high. The Pantheon was originally built for a church, and was used for that purpose for many years, but is now a monument of architecture of over a century gone by. The interior is simple and exceedingly bare, the walls are ornamented with mammoth paintings on canvas, that are fastened to the walls by means of white lead. They represent scenes of an historic nature. Above these are elaborate friezes in oil, artistic in design. In the basement are the old burial vaults, where formerly were buried Voltaire, Marat, Mirabeau and others, but their bodies were afterwards removed. The latest addition here is that of the remains of Sadi Carnot, the late President of the Republic, who was assassinated in 1894. The Pantheon was in the hands of the Commune for two days in May, 1871, and Milliére, one of the principal leaders, was shot dead upon the front steps.

Paris is full of Americans — I believe I made this statement once before. It is rather interesting to notice to what degree they will go in sight-seeing over here — what places they will visit, not only in Paris, but in all their European travels, that they would not think of visiting at home. There are many attractions of a more interesting nature right at their own doors, which they have never seen, or would never think of going to see. Verily, the Yankee is a curious bird, almost as much so as his English cousin.

Paris is full of "guides." One cannot step fifty feet from his hotel but he is spotted and asked if he wants to "see the sights." In most cases these guides will tell you they are American citizens, or lived in New York. They appeal to you as Americans. But beware of them; they are only "coppers" so to speak. They will charge you a fee for taking you around, and receive a big commission on whatever you buy, and you will pay double for everything you purchase under their direction. Here is a copy of a card one of them passed to me while I was there:

PHILIPS EXCURSION.

PARIS BY NIGHT.

Music Halls, Balls, Special Shows, Night Cafes, Different Sights.

Starting every evening at 8.30 from 18 Rue de la Paix.

FARE, 10 SHILLINGS EACH.

Admittances, Drinks, Fees and Everything Included.

Nothing to pay in advance.   No extra charges.

This was cheap enough for an "excursion" of that kind, for one Boston man who was here told me that he went out with a party of five, and it cost them $75 for about two hours' "sight-seeing." There was another inducement in the above, "drinks free."

Paris, yes, France, may well be proud of her Opera House. I say France, because the opera here is a government affair, owned and controlled by the same. The building was commenced in 1861 and completed in 1874, and is the largest amusement hall in the world. It covers an area of 122,364 square feet, or 13,596 square yards—nearly three acres. Yet it only contains a seating capacity for 2156 persons, for the reason that nearly all the gallery room except the top tier, is given up to private boxes. The land and building cost over $14,000,-000, and the building cannot be surpassed for its lavish decorations and magnificent finish. Entering the gilded gates, the visitor passes to the grand staircase, built of marble, thirty-two feet wide. The floor is divided into an orchestra, pit and amphitheatre, with a row of boxes on each side; the first, second and third galleries are entirely of boxes, the first and second rows belonging to subscribers and cannot be sold, the third tier only are offered the public. The fourth gallery contains the cheapest seats, which cost from sixty cents to $1.50 each. The stage is 196 feet high, 178 feet wide and 74 feet deep. A grand indoor and balcony promenade runs the entire width of the building. Opera is given every night during the season. Off season, and during the summer months, it must be given at least three times a week. Each night when the opera is open, a horse guard, mounted on a charger, stands in front of the main entrance, and a guard paces up and down the top landing of the front, while guards or soldiers are stationed at each entrance, and your tickets must be shown to them before you can pass in. Once in, soldiers are to be found in charge, and "old women" ushers show you your seats. One of the latter entered the box in which I sat, and asked me if I would be kind enough to give her a tip. An orchestra of seventy-five pieces furnishes the music, included in this are thirty-one violins. The opera at Paris is indeed a grand treat to an American visiting that city. Speaking on this subject, why would it not be a grand idea for the United States government to foster something of this kind at our national capital? If we do it, we want to do it well. If France can afford it, certainly we ought to be able to do so.

The Captain and I were walking along the street one day, when we noticed a large number of vacant stores with a sign in the same reading, "*A Louer*," meaning "To Let." The Captain, after we had passed a number, remarked, "That fellow, A. Louer, owns more stores than any other man in Paris."

I asked the Captain if he would not join me in a Turkish bath.

The Trocadero Palace and Gardens lie directly opposite the Eiffel Tower, just across the Seine. The palace is in the form of a crescent and is a magnificent structure. It is surmounted by a dome 173 feet in diameter, exceeding that of St. Peter's at Rome by 35 feet, and that of St. Paul's at London by 65 feet. The palace contains important salons devoted to sculptures and curiosities. On the Seine front is what at a distance resembles a great stairway but is a cascade on which the water is run at certain periods, the whole presenting a very fine effect.

The Gobelins were formerly the royal tapestry works and are now the property of the Republic. The origin of these works dates back to 1450. The tapestries manufactured here are the finest produced

Interior of Grand Opera House, Paris.

in the world. In some cases it takes several years to complete a particular design, and some of the productions cost as high as 50,000 francs, or $10,000. The works are usually copies of well-known pictures. These choice productions have for a number of generations been reserved for the exclusive use of the royal family for the time being, or have been presented to foreign courts, ambassadors or persons of distinction. At the present time only about 150 workmen are employed here.

Close to the Boulevard St. Germain, at the point where it is crossed by the Boulevard St. Michael, is the Musee de Cluny, or the Cluny Museum. On this spot there once stood an ancient Roman palace with baths, which the early Frankish kings continued to occupy until they removed into the city. The present building was erected by the Benedictine monks at the close of the fifteenth century, and is a fine example of the late gothic style. The museum is one of the most valuable in France and contains upwards of 9000 objects.

If you buy any article in Paris and ask for a bill, you are generally required to pay two cents extra for receipting it. The receipt is either by stamp or machine, the latter being used in large houses, and is automatic and furnished by the government. The revenue from this belongs to the Republic.

An interesting place is the Couciergerie. It was here that most of the political prisoners of the first Revolution were confined before being taken to execution. Marie Antoinette was confined here. The chamber occupied by her was afterward converted into a chapel, but was destroyed by the Commune of 1871. By an act of justice, Robespierre and the other butchers of the first Revolution were consigned here. In 1833, Prince Jerome Napoleon, and in 1890, the Duke of Orleans were imprisoned here for a short time.

" Do you know what is French for dirty?" asked the Captain.

My reply was that "*soille*" would cover the ground, and I asked the Captain why he inquired.

"Two or three times I have wanted a clean napkin and have had some difficulty in making the waiter understand me," was the reply.

I let the matter pass from my mind, at least for the time. It might have been a week later, that we—the Captain and myself—were seated at lunch, when I noticed him beckon to the waiter, and as he came up the Captain said :

The Pantheon, Paris.

"*Sortie.*"

"*Que, Monsieur?*" answered the waiter.

"*Sortie,*" again returned the Captain, so I was obliged to come to his relief, and asked him what he wanted.

"A clean napkin," was his reply.

"But why did you say '*Sortie*'?" I asked.

"I meant my napkin was dirty," said the Captain.

"But '*Sortie*' does not signify dirty. It means 'to go out,' or 'exit,'" I replied.

The Captain insisted that was the translation I had given him for dirty.

What could I do?

Why, like all newspaper men, I was forced to give in.

CHAPTER XIII.

Versailles and Fontainebleau.

IT IS the custom in Paris to give your cabman a tip. It is called *pour boire*, or drink money, and usually consists of twenty-five centimes, or five cents United States money. The Captain and myself had come in from a short ride one day, and the Captain handed the driver the regular fare, and was about to enter the hotel, when that individual hailed him and shouted, "*Pour Boire.*"

"Poor boy," answered the Captain, "well, I am sorry for you, here is a quarter." and he handed the man a franc. No sooner did *cocher* receive it than he whipped up his horse and got out of sight, as he evidently thought the Captain would repent of his generosity and recall the gift.

Twelve miles southwest from Paris lies the most interesting spot in France, Versailles. It is an easy carriage or coach drive of two hours, and the road lies through the Bois de Boulogne, St. Cloud and beautiful country suburbs dotted with fine groves and villas with flower gardens that make one feel as if he were in Paradise. Previous to the reign of Louis XIII., Versailles was used as a hunting ground. About 1624 that monarch became tired of the court residence, then St. Germain, and determined to build a palace that would command the admiration of all Europe Louis XIII. died in 1643, when his successor, Louis XIV., was but 5 years old, consequently the young king's mother, Anne of Austria, became Queen Regent, and the new court resided at Paris and St. Germain. Versailles was abandoned until 1662, when Louis XIV. was 24 years old. Liking Versailles very much he decided to enlarge the building and grounds and from that time to 1682 the place underwent great changes, when the king fixed his permanent residence here. In the meantime, the surrounding country to the extent of nearly fifty square miles was purchased, and when finished the undertaking is said to have cost over $100,000,000. Yet you are told, as you are shown through the palaces, that the expense was so enormous that before he died Louis XIV. destroyed all the books and accounts of this great undertaking, and the actual outlay was never known.

Louis XIV. disliked the French capital, Paris. In his new home with his mistresses he found life far more to his taste. He wanted to have assembled at Versailles and under his eye all the nobility of France, for they had caused him much trouble, but under this new régime he proposed to make them obey, therefore, it is said that there were in the palace and dependent upon it more than 10,000 people.

Louis XV., after the death of his predecessor, made some further changes and additions to the palace and grounds, including a very fine theatre, and several elegant apartments were fitted up, so Versailles continued to be the seat of government until 1789. The enormous amount of money that this place cost and the expense of keeping it up impoverished France and was, no doubt, the cause of the first Revolution in 1789. At the opening of this war the rich furniture was sold regardless of cost and was scattered here and there. What was not sold was destroyed by the mobs. Fortunately, however, during all the troublesome times, the palaces and parks were preserved and remain today a monument of the past folly of a great people and yet a delight to the civilized people of the present time. During the Empire it was intended to demolish the buildings and rebuild them in the Greek-Roman style. A competition was opened, but the expense was so great that Napoleon I. abandoned it. From 1815 to 1830 Louis XVIII. restored and repaired the place and it was inhabited by certain former servants of the Bourbons, but one can judge who and what they were, when we are told they hung their washing out of the windows to dry and kept cows and goats on the roof.

The evening after we returned from Versailles we visited the *Cirque d'Ete* on the Champ d'Elysees. The first part of the performance was very good, while the second part was a burlesque, entitled "Barkinson's Circus." In this act there were two performers, one made up evidently to represent a monkey and the other one to do the introducing. The Captain was very much interested, but was more surprised when he heard the performer shout something like this :

Palace at Versailles, Near Paris.

"*Allez-vous a travers la.*" Then burst out in English : "What's the matter with you?"

This thing kept up for some time, the man speaking a few words in French, but a good deal more in English. When he came up near the edge of the ring, where sat the Captain and myself, turning to me, the Captain remarked :

" I will bet you two dollars that fellow is a Yankee."

Imagine our surprise when the performer turned round and bowing to us, remarked :

" Right you are."

And the Captain was so delighted that had I not stopped him, I think he would have thrown his watch at the man.

I will not attempt to describe the gardens of Versailles. I could not do it justice. It is one of those places that must be seen to be appreciated. Enormous in extent, grandeur and beauty and a paradise in all. I might mention that here is the celebrated orange tree which was planted by Leonora, wife of Charles III., King of Navarre, who planted it in 1421, and now, after 475 years, it is still alive and in the height of vigor. The terrace is adorned with flower beds and two fountains, known as the Crowns and the Pyramids. Below the basin of the Pyramids are the Baths of Diana, and north of this lie the basins of Neptune and the Dragon. The former is the largest and most beautiful fountain in the world. It cost over $300,000 and is only played on state or special occasions as it costs $2000 to play it for less than half an hour. The other fountain plays every other Sunday during the summer.

At the extremity of the park is the beautiful villa known as Le Grand Trianon, built by Louis XIV. for his favorite mistress, Madame de Maintenon. The apartments are fitted up very fine and were occupied by the Dukes of Orleans and Nemours and before them by Napoleon I. They were intended to be used by Queen Victoria, during her proposed visit to Louis Philippe. In the Cabinet de la Reine is the bed formerly occupied by Josephine. This villa was a favorite resort for Louis XIV., Louis XV., Louis XVI. and also Napoleon I. The decorations are rich and abound in rare paintings and pieces of sculpture.

From here one goes to the Petit Trianon, the stable in which all the state carriages are kept. Here are shown four sleds owned by

Louis XIV., the carriage used by Napoleon as First Consul, the one used at the coronation of Charles XII.; and the one used by the King of Rome and for the marriage of Napoleon III. and Eugenie, also the state carriage built expressly for the Czar of Russia on his visit to Paris in 1896.

The Petit Trianon was built by Louis XV. for his mistress, Madame du Barri. The building is 70 feet square. The place is small in comparison with the other buildings. In the garden is a pretty little theatre, also a Swiss cottage erected for Marie Antoinette.

Entering the large palace of Versailles, we pass through the gallery of statuary, which is very fine, the most notable piece being that of Joan of Arc, by the late Princess Maria of Wurtemburg. In the Salle de Constantine are to be seen many fine pictures and from here we pass to the Salle de l'Opera, where performances formerly took place. Attached to the royal box of the theatre is the Foyer du Roi, where the court formerly partook of refreshments between the acts. In this hall, in 1855, a grand banquet was given in honor of the visit of Queen Victoria. Close to the theatre is a gallery of statues and busts that is interesting, and near by a salon devoted to pictures of battles fought during the Crusade in the Holy Land. The next interesting place is the gallery of Louis Philippe, which contains a collection of historical paintings of the Revolution up to 1830, and from here we approach what is known as the grand apartments, and which occupy all the part of that first floor of the central projection which faces the garden. Those on the north were occupied by the king, and those on the south by the queen. The ornamentations are paintings illustrating the life of Louis XIV. One of the salons contains the "Three Graces" of Pradier. The Salon de Mars was formerly used as a ballroom, and adjoining this was what was once the state bedroom, which contains a beautiful ceiling painted by Philippe of Champagne. The Throne room comes next. When Queen Victoria visited here this was used as the ballroom and was a scene of great brilliancy. The ball was opened with a quadrille, the Emperor leading with Queen Victoria.

From the Throne room we pass to what is called the most beautiful room in the world, known now as the Grande Galerie de Louis XIV., and 242x35 feet and 43 feet high. The ceiling is a work of art, while the walls are ornamented with red marble Corinthian pilasters. There are four niches in which are statues of Venus, Adonis, Mercury and Minerva. To the left of this are the private or reserved apartments of the king. It was from the windows of one of these apartments that the royal family were accustomed to sit to watch the return of the hunters from the chase. The handsomest room of all the apartments is the bedroom of Louis XIV., and the bed in which he died is still there. The decorations are superb. Pictures of the royal family hang on the walls. From here we pass to the chamber of Marie Antoinette, which was successively occupied by three queens named Marie, Maria Theresa, queen of Louis XIV., Maria Leczinska, queen of Louis XV., and Marie Antoinette, queen of Louis XVI. On the night of Oct. 5, 1789, Marie Antoinette was asleep in this room when the mob broke into the palace, and she made her escape through a small corridor leading to the grand antechamber of the king

We next visit the magnificent Salon du Sacre, which contains David's celebrated picture of "The Coronation of Napoleon," painted at a cost of $20,000. From here we pass to one of the most interesting rooms in the palace, the Salle de 1782, which contains portraits of all the heroes of the Revolution of 1789. In the Escalier des Princes are three fine marble statues of Napoleon I., Louis Philippe and Louis XIV., and at the foot of the stairs is the Napoleon salon, containing statues and busts of the Napoleon family.

The Grande Galerie des Batailles is, in my opinion, the finest salon I ever entered. It is magnificent, over 400 feet long, and devoted to mammoth paintings of battles in which the French people took part, from the fifth to the nineteenth century, and among them was the Battle of Yorktown in the American Revolution, with a life size picture of Washington. It will be remembered that in this fight the French took an active part in behalf of the American forces. From here we go to the Attique du Midi, a suite of rooms devoted to historical portraits, where the American visitor will recognize those of Henry Clay, Andrew Jackson, Daniel Webster and James K. Polk. It is interesting to know that they are in the famous palace at Versailles. The tour is closed with a view of several other salons, one containing portraits of all the kings of France from Pharamond to Louis Philippe.

Versailles is indeed a great place to visit, and one that will make a lasting impression on the visitor.

The Great Fountain at Versailles.

Returning from Versailles, a stop was made at Sevres Porcelain Works owned by the government and located in the town of that name. In 1759, at the earnest solicitation of Madame de Pompadour, Louis XV. bought these works, and they have since been operated by the state. The product is the finest of its kind in the world and is very costly. To own a piece of Sevres is like owning something that your friends and neighbors do not have or cannot get. Fine show rooms are opened to the public, and the process of manufacturing is shown and explained. It is an interesting place to visit.

The Captain took a seat in a barber shop one afternoon to have a shave. It is the custom here to shave only and let the customer wash his face. The Captain leaned back as well as he could in the straight back chair, and was duly shaved or, as he called it, "scraped." In the meantime he had closed his eyes, while I was busily engaged in reading a paper. The barber had completed his work and passed to another customer, while the Captain slept on and I read my paper. Looking up, after some time, I discovered the condition of things and awoke the Captain. When I explained the situation the Captain fell back in his chair, remarking that he had not made any trade as to price, and was going to have a shave and clean up or sit there all day. I notified the barber that he had better get a move on and finish up the Captain or there would be trouble. So the job was completed, and when the Captain asked the price and was told thirty centimes, or six cents, he rather knocked out the boss of the shop and all his jours when he gave the man one franc (twenty cents) as he departed.

Fontainebleau! What a history has Fontainebleau! What tales its walls could unfold were they gifted with the power of speech!

The palace of Fontainebleau was erected in 1547, by Francis I., and was considered of almost unparalleled extent and magnificence. The exterior is only two stories high, and it is less imposing, compared with many other noted buildings of this character, than one would suppose. It is the interior that enchants the visitor. It was decorated by French and Italian artists, and is much admired. Henry IV. made considerable additions to it, but it has undergone but few changes since his time, except being restored at a large expense by Louis Philippe and Napoleon III. There are several historic associations connected with the palace beside those of which

Palace at Fontainebleau, Near Paris.

mention will be made. Henry IV. caused his companion in arms, Marshal Biron, to be arrested here on a charge of high treason on June 4, 1602, and a month later had him beheaded. Louis XIV. signed the revocation of the Edict of Nantes here in 1685, by which Henry IV. had granted toleration to the Protestants in 1598, and it was here that Napoleon I. secured his divorce from Josephine in 1809.

An hour by express train from Paris and you are at Fontainebleau. The palace and grounds are reached by carriage in fifteen minutes. The place is open to visitors throughout the year, and it will require only one day to make the trip, inspect the buildings and return home. The buildings are divided in five different courts. The first, the Cour du Cheval Blanc, is the largest, and was the scene of Napoleon's parting from the grenadiers of his Old Guard, on April 20, 1814, after his abdication. It was also here that he viewed the same troops before marching them to Paris, on the 20th of March, 1815.

On the ground floor is the Chapelle de la Trinité, where Louis XV. was married in 1725 and the Duc d'Orleans in 1837. Napoleon III. was baptized here in 1810. From here a broad stairway leads to the apartments of Napoleon I. In this room is to be seen Napoleon's bed, a clock ornamented with cameos given to Napoleon by Pius VII., and furniture brought from Marie Antoinette's apartments at the Trianon. To the left of this is the Salle du Conceil, or council chamber, and following we arrive at the boudoir of Marie Antoinette, with some historic furniture therein.

The Galerie de Diane, a hall 265 feet long, and constructed under the direction of Henry IV., is adorned with elegant paintings, representing mythological scenes and a library of about 35,000 volumes. In this room, in 1657, Queen Christina, of Sweden, was a guest of the French court after her abdication, and caused her unfortunate and favorite Count Monaldeschi to be put to death after a pretended trial for treason. The Salons de Reception, or reception rooms, are handsomely embellished with Gobelin tapestry. The Salon Louis XIII. is the one in which that king was born.

The Salles de St. Louis contain fifteen pictures relating to the life of Henry IV. In the Salon aux Jeux is a clock of Louis XIV. The Salles des Gardes is the last of the suite, and is adorned with a fine bust of Henry IV. There are other apartments less interesting, but there are two fine halls, one the Galerie d'Henry II., which is 100x33 feet, and the other the Galerie de Francis I., 210x20 feet. Both are embellished with paintings, etc. To the left of the Vestibule d'Honneure are the apartments of Reines Méres and Pius VII. They were once occupied by Catherine de Medicis, Anne of Austria, mother of Louis XIV., and later by Pius VII., who was a prisoner from June, 1812, to January, 1814. A number of other rooms follow, showing the bedrooms of Anne of Austria and Pius VII. and the Galerie des Assiettes, which derives its name from the quaint style in which it was decorated, by order of Louis Philippe, with plates of porcelain bearing views of royal residences.

The gardens of Fontainebleau are fine, and well worth the trip. The Avenue Maintenon leads to the forests of Fontainebleau, and the decorations of the gardens are all told in the story of the early days of the French Empire. The forests of Fontainebleau adjoin, and are about fifty miles in circumference and cover about 42,000 acres. This is regarded as the most beautiful place of its kind in all France. Volumes have been written in which Fontainebleau and its forests have been the central figure. It is a grand place, and after a tour of its courts the average visitor is filled with a desire to study carefully the history of France. It will be found much more interesting reading than two-thirds of the novels of the present generation.

The Captain accompanied me to the Louvre Art Gallery, Paris, and appeared to be interested in the display. After passing through the various salons, we took our way to the basement, where was a great exhibition of statuary. This captured the Captain, and he examined every subject carefully until he came to the Venus de Milo, when he stopped short.

"Come," said he, "let us get out of here."

"Why?" I asked.

"Because, this place is a fraud."

"A fraud," I answered, "why, my dear Captain, this is one of the great art galleries of Europe; why do you say it is a fraud?"

"Just look at that statue of that woman, both arms gone. I say this is a fraud."

And the Captain pushed his hat on the back of his head and strolled toward a looking-glass near by, arranged his necktie and said he was ready to go.

We went.

In how many ways has the old proverb, "Tall oaks from little acorns grow," been observed in business enterprises! To the visitor to Paris one of the first sights in the way of commercial enterprises is the "Louvre Magazine," or, as we would put it, the great department store of the Louvre. Parisians are proud of this great establishment, and it is as well known to the regular visitor here as it is to the resident. Located directly at the foot of the Avenue de l'Opera, it is within walking distance of all the great hotels, or only a few minutes' ride in a cab or an omnibus.

In 1855, two men who had spent some years in a commercial way founded the Louvre. They were Messrs. Alfred Chauchard and Auguste Heriot. This was a period in which France was beginning to make a stride forward. It was at this time that a great wave of industrial prosperity rolled over the country. The first universal Exposition was in progress; the Emperor Napoleon III. cut through and opened up that splendid thoroughfare, the Rue de Rivoli, and other improvements were made that commenced that transformation in Paris that has since made it known as the most beautiful city in the world. Great railroads were at this time in process of construction, and the people of the empire who had been so isolated from each other began to realize that they were closer together as a nation. In the midst of all these advantages the Louvre Magazine was opened to the public, and it was certainly an event that is remembered to this day by the older inhabitants.

The proprietors Messrs. Chauchard and Heriot, brought to their enterprise not only a force of organization but a surety of taste that made it a gigantic success. From the first it was their motto to insure square dealing and honesty in all transactions, not only with their customers but with their help as well, and thus build up a strong organization, for they both had something better in view than the present. In the first place, they adopted a fixed or one price system and bought their goods in large quantities. In case goods were purchased and after they were taken home not liked, they could be returned and exchanged, or the money refunded, thus securing one of the greatest boons in a business career, the confidence of their trade.

In August, 1879, Mr. Heriot died, and in 1885 Mr. Chauchard retired from active business, in the enjoyment of a large fortune

made by a long and honorable business career. He has, since giving up his active business life, devoted large sums to the encouragement of the arts and donated to various philanthropic societies, besides keeping his old clerks who had been his working companions in his prosperous days. Thus the Louvre Magazine passed from the hands of its founders to the present directors, who have made it a study to follow out the same lines which has made this great establishment what it is. Every facility is offered their customers which they can possibly carry out, such as free delivery in Paris, and the same outside of the city on purchases amounting to a certain sum. They are alive in advertising, and have a department for this purpose, and issue catalogues, etc., which they distribute all over the country. In order to contribute to the development, taste and beauty of their models the house usually offers prizes, to which are invited master workmen and manufacturers who are interested in art as applied to industry.

For their employes the directors of the Louvre take special care. They have for their benefit a mutual aid society, a department of beneficence, a department of medical assistance, not only for their aid while active, but for those who through overwork need a rest and sea air or baths. A place is provided for the latter free of all expense. In order to bring their large family together as much as possible (and it is policy to do this, as over 3000 people are employed in this vast establishment) they have two lodging houses, one for men and the other for women, where they are given free lodging. The Louvre Magazine is closed at 7 o'clock every evening, so as to allow their help the advantages of some time to themselves. Everything is done to encourage the study of foreign languages, for the store is thronged daily with people from all countries. A school has been established for this purpose, and every year a purse is presented to certain ones, to enable them to travel abroad and learn the manners and customs, as well as assist them in the language of the people. I met one gentleman there who had been a resident of Boston for over two years, employing his time in perfecting himself in English.

In order to encourage economy a department of current accounts, or banking room, has been opened, where deposits are received up to 5000 francs ($1000), on which interest at the rate of four per cent is paid. In order to recompense in a measure for long service, gold medals are given annually to all who have served twenty-five years with the house, and if any of the help is called out for military duty they are reinstated on their return.

While being conducted through the Louvre Magazine, I was taken to the dining rooms and kitchens on the top floor. Here over three thousand people are fed daily. A nominal charge of 150 centimes, or thirty cents United States currency, is made to cover the bare cost of the food. For this they receive two meals per day, breakfast and dinner, and good meals they are, including a bottle of wine at each. The kitchen was as large as that of the greatest hotel in the land.

Let me commend the methods of this great establishment to our American merchants, and let me say: "Try and do likewise." If you ever visit Paris give this great establishment a call. You will be welcomed, and see a sight worth going many miles to see.

One evening the Captain came rushing into the reading room of our hotel at Paris and taking hold of the lapel of my coat, urged me to follow him.

"What's up, Captain?" I asked

"Come here," he said, "come here. A fellow has insulted me, and I propose to lick him."

"What is the trouble, Captain?"

"It's just this," he replied, "I was out riding, and when I came in the driver called me a sow."

"Called you what?" I answered.

"A sow, did you ever hear of such impudence?"

And the Captain, who was rather stout, actually unbuttoned his collar to give him easy use of his neck.

I thought there must be some mistake, so I prevailed upon my friend to remain where he was until I investigated the matter. I found the hackman still in front of the hotel, and when I talked with him I learned he had asked the Captain for a few sous (a sou is one cent). I gave the man what he asked for and, returning to the Captain, explained his mistake. He declared he was sick and tired of a country that made such use of the English language.

CHAPTER XIV.

Last Days in the Gay French Capital.

ONE beautiful morning, as I came down from my room in my hotel at Paris, I was met by the Captain, who greeted me with his usual smile and turning to me, remarked,

"*Bon marche, monsieur.*"

I stopped for a moment and looked at the Captain, wondering what he meant, for *Bon marche* in French means cheap, or low priced, but I thought I would flatter him a little and turning to him, I remarked:

"You are improving in your French, Captain."

"Yes," was his reply. "I have been in Paris now nearly two weeks, and I think if I should stay here two weeks longer, *I would make a good Parasite.*"

Later on, I learned that the Captain intended to say to me,—"*Bon matin, monsieur,*" meaning, "Good morning, sir."

It is a pity that man's life is not spared to a greater number of years to enjoy the workings of a great enterprise that he has established. Yet the great Giver of all things has decided otherwise. While I was in Paris I could not help sauntering, or rather taking a cab drive, over to that great, yes, that marvelous store, the Bon Marché. Everyone who goes to Paris visits this place. Everyone who does not go there must have heard of it. Here, gathered together under one roof, is the most interesting store in the world. It is a department house, yet it is not a grocery establishment, nor a Cheap John affair. It is a place where the best, as well as the cheaper grade of goods can be found, yet the aim of the management is to dispose of these at the very lowest cash prices that they can possibly be sold.

In 1853 Aristide Boucicaut was a partner in a druggist's business in Paris. Of this house up to 1863 but little is on record. However,

Monsieur Boucicaut had in the meantime secured a portion of this world's goods, so that in the last named year he purchased the interest of his partners and became the sole proprietor of the business. At this time the business was a comparatively small one; Monsieur Boucicaut was blessed in having for a wife an energetic lady, whose sole aim was that of her husband's future success, and it was partially through her efforts that this great establishment is what it is at the present day. One of the first things Monsieur Boucicaut did was to study carefully the interest of his people; he sought to make the lives of those in his employ happier and more pleasant, and to make them feel as if they were part of a family rather than servants. This soon attracted the attention of the general public, and, like all patriotic Frenchmen and French women, they were not slow in showing their appreciation of this philanthropist, and he began to receive his reward in a substantial way.

Six years alone in business is but a short time when one has the many cares of an enterprise that each year shows rapid gains, but in that time, or in 1869, Monsieur Boucicaut found he must have a larger store, and the corner stone of the present Bon Marché building was laid. When the great structure was completed and ready for occupancy it seems that renewed prosperity came to Monsieur Boucicaut, for the business increased at a wonderful rate.

To attempt to describe the floors and the many departments of the Bon Marché would be impossible. It would be so lengthy that it would be tiresome, but in order to give some idea of the magnitude of this establishment the illustrations presented on other pages have been prepared. The store occupies one entire square or block. It is located on the left bank of the Seine, beyond the Latin quarter. It is easily accessible from any part of Paris by a system of omnibuses, trams and cabs. Go there when you will and you will always find a vast crowd of purchasers.

Monsieur Boucicaut not only showed his ability as a business man and a manager, but his success was largely due to the spirit of enterprise, the honesty of purpose and the way he conducted his affairs and his great benevolences. Therefore, he not only founded a great and powerful business, but a great humane work, a social institution. He gathered around him a staff of competent and superior employes. These he chose with care and made them understand that his interests were their interests. One of the first things he did was to provide a Provident Fund, and this was followed by Madame Boucicaut founding a Retiring Pension Fund, which guaranteed to all the old employes of the house ample relief when they reached old age, and were rendered incapable of attending to business demands.

Upon the death of Monsieur Boucicaut some years ago, his wife arranged so as to allow the most competent employes to purchase stock in the concern and thus become financially interested. The moral and intellectual condition of the army of people employed here has been carefully looked after. Free evening classes for the study of English, vocal and instrumental music, and fencing were formed and largely attended. Each year those who show the most rapid development of English are sent to London for a period of six months to study up this branch, and all expenses are paid by the house. The Bon Marché has interpreters for all languages, rendered necessary on account of the large number of foreigners who visit the store while in Paris. A picture and sculpture gallery is a feature of the place, where artists are allowed to display their works and find possible customers. Only originals are received, copies not being allowed in the gallery. In case a visitor finds a picture he or she may like, and an offer is made for the same, this is submitted to the artist, and if accepted the sale is made, and the entire amount paid over to the artist, as no charge or commission is taken by the establishment.

To show the benevolent workings of the Bon Marché I give some idea of the magnitude of the same. The Boucicaut Provident Fund, established in 1876, is supported by means of a sum deducted annually from the profits of the business, and may be summed up as follows: In 1876 there was in this fund 62,020 francs, or about $12,500. In 1886 there was 1,009,130 francs, or about $200,000, and in 1897 there is about 2,500,000 francs or about $500,00. All help employed by the house for five years become participators in its benefit. Each participant has an individual account opened in his or her name and is provided with a book indicating exactly the amount lying to his credit. This account is annually increased by interest at the rate of four per cent per annum. The right of obtaining the capital to their credit is as follows: By all lady assistants who have served fifteen years in the employ of the firm, or who reach the age of forty-five years; by all men who have been in the employ of the house for

Bois de Boulogne, Paris.

twenty years, or reached the age of fifty years. In case of death, all accounts standing to the credit of those interested are transferred or paid to husband or wife, or children, or direct legal heirs, irrespective of time, age or service. In addition to the amount of capital of this fund in 1897 there has already been paid out 1,000,000 francs, or $200,000.

The Employes' Pension Fund, created by Madame Boucicaut in 1886, started with a fund of 5,000,000 francs, or $1,000,000, given by Madame Boucicaut from her personal fortune. This capital now amounts to nearly 7,000,000 francs, or $1,400,000 and 130 people who have formerly been in the employ of the house, have retired and are receiving pensions amounting in all to 110,000 francs per year, or about $22,000. All employes in the Bon Marché who have served it for twenty years, or men who reach fifty years, and women who reach forty-five years, are entitled to receive benefit from this fund. It is a life pension, and varies from 600 francs ($120) to 1500 francs ($300) per year.

Employes who are obliged to leave the house for military duty are reinstated when their time expires. They are obliged to give notice of their desire to return and present an irreproachable military certificate. If summoned out by the government for a month or less duty, they are allowed two francs (40 cents) per day and 1 franc (20 cents) per day for each of their children during the short time they are out. A doctor is engaged by the house for the help and free service given.

Both Monsieur and Madame Boucicaut have gone to their reward, and their successors show by their works that they have at heart the great principles left them by the founders of Bon Marché. In addition to the benefits already described, they started in 1892 a second pension and benefit fund, to be devoted exclusively to the workpeople engaged in the workrooms of the Bon Marché, and happiness and prosperity has attended them in their efforts to make those around them believe that life is worth living.

A French gentleman was explaining to the Captain the Franco-Russian alliance, and was quite enthusiastic about the combination made by the two countries. "The flags of these two countries," he remarked, "are as near one as ever such an arrangement was known in all Europe, and we can stand or fall together."

The Captain paused for a moment, I knew something was coming, but it came quicker than I thought, when he replied :

"Yes, I suppose you feel secure, but we own a **flag** on the other side of the great Atlantic that stands—or flies—alone. **The Stars and Stripes** can look out for itself, and needs no alliance."

It is amusing to hear the cry that goes up from the American tourists **about** the effect of the new tariff bill on their personal baggage. The trouble is mostly with the feminine portion. **And** I have thought to myself, "What fools **these** mortals **be.**" **I was** talking with one gentleman who appeared delighted at the **good news he** had heard **from his** beloved home across the sea. Business promised well. **It had** not promised so well **for nearly five years.** He **was** a man **of means, and owned a considerable amount in stocks. These had advanced in value, and I judged from what I gathered from the conversation that, taking all** things together, this man **would be better off by four or five thousand** dollars before the new **year came in.** That same afternoon I met his wife. She was raging mad, she almost swore. I believe if she had had the present administration at her mercy in Paris she would have annihilated the whole lot, and all this because she had bought seven or eight hundred dollars' worth of goods, and would have to pay duty on all but one hundred dollars. I judge she would be taxed about one hundred and fifty dollars. When I compared the report given me by her husband and her own feelings, I thought with the maker of the remark, "Consistency thou art a jewel." This, however, is only a sample. People who earn their money in the United States, should learn to spend it there. If they cannot find what they want here, and prefer to go abroad and spend their cash, let them pay for it.

One with plenty of leisure time on his hands often meets with queer experiences over here. I remember coming in contact with a gentleman and his wife from Philadelphia. I am of the opinion they were people well-to-do. They told me they paid eight hundred dollars each for their expenses for a three months' tour over here. That was sixteen hundred dollars for the pair. They brought with them fifteen hundred dollars to spend, and the moment they landed in a town they would make a bee line for the stores. The sacred attractions were neglected; art galleries, great cathedrals and the wonders of nature were "not in it." They had no attraction for this pair. It was the shops, the shop windows and the displays they made. And this man delighted in telling me that he never paid the prices asked him, but always beat the storekeepers down. I don't know as I can blame him much for that, as the shopkeepers of Europe have learned to charge as high a price as possible, and—take what they can get. The smart shopper has found it to be so.

I was passing along one of the boulevards with the Captain, when his attention was attracted by a large sign over a store that read, '*Confections pour Dames.*'

"Come in here a moment with me," said the Captain.

We entered the store, and as the attendant came forward the Captain said, "Give me one pound of your best chocolates."

"*Comment, monsieur,*" was the reply.

Before the Captain could answer, I told the waiting clerk it was a mistake, and got my companion outside.

"Why did you go in there and ask for chocolate creams?" I asked.

"Because I wanted them," was the reply.

"But why did you go in such a store as this? They do not keep confectionery here, but ladies' made-up garments," I returned.

"Look at that sign over the door," said the Captain "'*Confections for Dames*,' isn't that plain enough?"

And when I told the Captain that 'confections' in French meant made-up garments for ladies' wear, he said he was sick of a country whose early education had been so sadly neglected.

One of the greatest nuisances of European travel is the gauntlet one has to run at the hotels, depots and about every place where you are at the mercy of others. If you do not tip these people they are ready to go for you. Here is a sample of my own experience at a certain place where I was. The day before my departure I notified the office of my intention to go, and ordered my bill to be ready. When I boarded my train I made a memorandum of what I was obliged to pay in tips, and here is a copy of it:

Head waiter at hotel,	$1.00
Two waiters each $2,	4.00
Chambermaid,	.50
Chambermaid assistant,	.50
Two elevator men, each 25c	.50
Porter,	1.00
Bootblack,	.75
Two office boys, each 50c	1.00
Bell boy,	.25
Door-keeper,	.50
Two porters for handling baggage, 25c	.50
Cab driver,	.10
Three depot porters, each 10c	.30
Total	$10.90

Room in the Cluny Museum, Paris.

The Captain got interested in a duel between Prince Henri d'Orleans and the Count of Turin.

"What's all this racket about?" he asked.

When I told him that the Count considered the Prince had insulted the Italian soldiers by claiming that they were cowards, the Captain replied :

"Do you know what I would do with these two fellows if I had my way? I would give them six months each for being drunk and disorderly, or send both to the insane asylum for their natural lives."

The Captain meant it.

About the dullest and toughest customer I ever had a tussle with was a Paris policeman. As the boy said, "They don't know beans " Ask one a question and ten to one you cannot get a reply. If you do you know about as much after they tell you as you did before. They are a stupid set, decidedly so. Not because I could not understand their French or they understand mine, but because they were not an accommodating set. Far different from the London "bobby," who will walk a block with you to give you the information you want—with, of course, the prospect of a tip.

Paris was full of American songs and American airs. The bands played them, the hurdy-gurdys played them, and they sang them in concert saloons. It seemed to me as if America had been moved over here for a while.

I have often heard arguments about the cost of living in Paris—I am not speaking of hotel, but private life. Some were of the opinion one could live cheaper here, while others thought it was more expensive. It is decidedly the latter. One can live cheaply here, if he or she elects. For instance, a room can be secured for four or five francs per week, breakfast at one franc, lunch at one and a half francs and dinner at two to three francs, making a total cost of room and three meals per day from $1 to $1.25. Mind you, this is the cheapest way a person of limited means could live, unless he went down to the slum methods. But what can you do at home? Say Boston, for instance. Room, $1 per week, board of three square meals at restaurant or dining rooms, $3.50 per week, total, $4.50 per week, or twenty-five per cent cheaper than in Paris, and a far better table. When one goes to the better class of houses and better class of cafés, the cost is far ahead of that here in our own country. In buying there are certain things favorable to both sides; for instance, kid gloves, silks, laces and clothing are cheaper here than in the United States, but there are enough things to offset these that are cheaper in our own land to make the balance in our favor. A French lady, born in Paris, told me that after a residence of a few years in Boston she was fully convinced that she could take one hundred dollars and buy more for it in Boston or New York than she could in Paris. Of course, she referred to women's necessities in dress.

I was invited to inspect a sensation in Paris known as the Café de la Morte, or the Café of Death. I was ushered into a room with rows of coffins on each side which served as tables and where refreshments were served. Here a series of pictures were hung on the walls, and shown by electric lights, changing from life to death scenes. Skulls and crossbones covered the place. Lighted tapers were given each person and a walk was taken to a hall where an exhibition of turning a live man into a skeleton in his own coffin was given, this was followed by an exhibition of ghosts in another hall, and we were told to "sortie."

Such is only a mild sample of life in the Parisian capital.

The Captain wanted to buy a pair of opera glasses, and was examining a certain pair in a store, and asked the price.

"Fifty francs, monsieur," was the reply.

"How much?" asked the Captain.

"Fifty francs, monsieur," came the answer.

"I won't pay it," was the reply. "I'll tell you what I'll do. I'll give you just ten dollars for them," remarked the Captain.

"Well, monsieur," answered the storekeeper. "I can't afford it, but you may take them."

When we got outside and I told the Captain that fifty francs was just ten dollars, he wanted me to go back with him while he offered the man five dollars. But it was too late; he had bought and paid for them, and I settled the matter satisfactorily by paying for the cigars.

CHAPTER XV.

Cambridge and Oxford.

MY ENDEAVORS to teach the Captain French were not particularly successful, but once in a while he remembered what I told him. One day he asked me what the French called England, and I told him *Angleterre*. When we crossed the Channel it was terribly rough and the Captain was one of the sickest of the entire ship's company. As we stepped off the gang-plank, I asked :

"Captain, aren't you glad to get on terra firma again ? "

The Captain looked at me for a moment, and then said :

"Look here, quit fooling with me. When I asked you what these Frenchmen called England you said *Angleterre*, now you call it Terra Firma. I may not know as much as you do, but I know terra firma is the stuff they adulterate candy with."

I gave it up.

I think, without exception, the most beautiful place I visited in England was Cambridge. Cambridge can be reached from London by express train in about one hour and forty minutes. The town is an old one, dating back beyond the Romans, and after the departure of these people, the Danes pillaged and burned the town in 870, and again in 1010. Of the subsequent history of Cambridge up to the time of the Norman Conquest, very little is known. William the Conqueror, having taken possession of it, founded the castle in 1068 and from it conducted his military operations against the Saxon prelates and nobles, who, with Hereward and his army, long held their camp of refuge at Ely. So obstinate was the resistance that in 1069 the king was obliged to come in person to Cambridge Castle, with a powerful army, in order to reduce these insurgents. In 1088 the town and county were laid waste with fire and sword by Roger de Montgomery, Earl of Shrewsbury, who was in arms in support of Robert Curthose, Duke of Normandy, the elder son of the Conqueror.

The town remained in the king's hands until the time of Henry I., the sheriffs of the county rendering the annual profits to the town's exchequer. But that prince granted to the burgesses the liberty to hold their town at farm, they paying to him the same sum as the sheriff of the county had been accustomed to render. Henry I., having been educated here, had a partiality for the place and in gratitude endowed readers of several languages therein. Besides, he ordered in 1118 that "no vessel should unlade or pay toll for its goods anywhere but in Cambridge." Fires, pestilence and frequent civil discord followed these events. The towns suffered from plunder, disputes and anarchy during the reign of the Plantaganet kings. In 1267, King Henry III., commenced to fortify the town to protect it against the rebellious barons. He caused a ditch to be made, surrounding it on those sides where it was not protected by the river. He partially built a wall, which was soon destroyed by the insurgents. He also erected two gates, all trace of which has since disappeared, but the ditch remains and it is still called the King's Ditch, although all but a small portion is covered over.

In 1381 a serious tumult rose between the townsmen and the University. The townsmen assembled at their hall and having chosen and obliged James de Grantcestre to act as their leader, they committed the most flagrant acts of violence. They broke open the doors of the Corpus Christi College, carried away the charters, jewels and other goods belonging to that institution. They obliged several of the masters to renounce, under pain of death and destruction of their dwellings, all the privileges that had ever been granted them. After this, they broke open the University chest in St. Mary's church and taking out all the records burned them, with the other papers, in the market place. Many other acts of violence accompanied these proceedings and the misguided crowd, to insure its own safety, forced certain of the principal members of the University to sign a bond which vested its entire future government in the burgesses of the town. Soon after, however, this usurped power was wrested from their hands by Henry le Spencer, Bishop of Norwich. Several of the principal leaders were imprisoned during life; the mayor was deprived of his office, and the liberties granted by King John and Henry III. were declared forfeited and part of them bestowed on the chancellor of the University.

In 1574 the town was visited by the plague. In 1643, Cromwell, who had twice represented the town, took possession of it for the Parliament and put in a garrison of 1000 men.

Many other interesting events took place, but from the restoration of the Stuarts to the present time there is scarcely anything to record concerning the history of Cambridge likely to interest the visitor.

The Captain was enjoying a smoke one evening, and had for a companion an English gentleman who had devoted many years to travel. In the course of the conversation, the Englishman was describing a trip up the Rhine.

"I suppose," he remarked, "that you Americans were delighted with the Rhine?"

"Yes," answered the Captain, "we are, but we do not call it by that name."

"You do not," replied the Captain's friend; "what do you call it?"

"We know it as the Danube river;" answered the Captain, as he endeavored to toss the ashes from his cigar, but in doing so they covered the dark trousers of his companion.

The origin and progress of the University would make a history in itself, and is said to have dated back as far as the seventh century, but it was towards the close of the thirteenth century, or in 1284, that the first institution at all answering to the present college foundation was erected. In that year, Hugh de Balshan, Bishop of Ely, purchased two hostels, near St. Mary's church, now called St. Mary's the Less, and placed scholars in them whom he endowed with certain possessions, thus making what is known as Peter's, or St. Peter's College. This plan seems to have been adopted in subsequent foundations. For the next 400 or 500 years the University went on increasing in wealth and magnificence, royal visits were frequently paid to it, and kings became its fathers and queens its nursing mothers. Special charters were granted to it, the earliest dating from the reign of Henry III. and many important privileges were conceded to it by succeeding monarchs, especially Edward III.

In 1614 James I. conferred upon the University the privilege of sending two members to Parliament, the right of election being vested in the members of the Senate.

The colleges are seventeen in number, to which have lately been added two hostels, one theological college, and two colleges for women, all independent and incorporate bodies; in fact, each college is an independent corporation, but all are subject to the paramount laws of the University, in the administration of which they all bear a share. The principal officer is the chancellor, whose power, however, is merely nominal and is delegated to a vice-chancellor. An annual election is held for the office of vice-chancellor, who is chosen from among the heads of the colleges. During his year of office he has the government of this literary commonwealth.

The public orator is another important officer. He acts as the mouthpiece of the Senate on all public occasions. Each college has its own master, or head; several fellows, who are maintained by the revenues of the foundation; scholars, who are students of superior attainments, elected by examination, who receive payments in money and other advantages; pensioners, or ordinary students, who pay their own expenses and derive no pecuniary advantage from the colleges, and sizars, who, being students of limited means, have both the University and college fees greatly reduced to them and receive various emoluments.

Most of the colleges lie on the right side of the river and are old structures with courtyards, cloisters, beautiful grass plots, with flower beds, etc., that are enchanting to the visitor. In the rear, across the river, is a magnificent wood with many shade trees and pathways. This is all kept up in excellent taste, the grass being green and well preserved and the road beds in perfect order; in fact, it almost makes one feel like going through fairyland. It is my purpose merely to mention a few of the colleges that I visited while there.

One day the Captain intended to visit a nearby town, and while taking a hurried lunch asked the waiter if he would make all possible speed, as he did not want to miss his train.

"We always accommodate our guests," was the reply, "and I am certain the railway will do likewise."

The Captain looked up to me and said: "There is civility for you. 'Where would you find that in America?'" And he gave his attendant a five shilling piece in mistake for a shilling.

Whether we regard the number of its members, the extent of its buildings, or the long roll of illustrious men who have been educated

Bridge of Sighs, St. John's College, Cambridge, England.

within its walls, Trinity College is the noblest collegiate foundation in the Kingdom of Great Britain. Christ's Church College is a larger one in extent of buildings, but falls considerably short of Trinity in standing.

Trinity College was formed by the consolidation and extension of several earlier foundations, dating back to that of the Michael House, founded in 1324, and several others of equal note. The entrance or gateway is worthy of special notice, and is one of the finest of its kind, and is known as the King's Gateway. It was built in the reign of Edward IV. The truth of this is proved by the fact that the royal arms on the outer front are supported by two lions, no other monarch having used these supporters. At the same time this gate was evidently intended for Edward III. for it is surrounded by the garter and the arms of France. On either side of the king's arms, under rich canopies, are those of the sons of Edward III., a blank shield being left for his second son, William of Hatfield, who died in infancy.

In a large niche between the windows is a statue of Henry VIII. On the inner side of the tower are statues of King James I., Anne of Denmark, his queen, and their eldest son, Henry, Prince of Wales. The roof beneath the gateway is modern, and is a handsome and ingenious example of wooden vaulting. It is ornamented with shields bearing the arms of all the masters of the college. Sir Isaac Newton stayed here, and his rooms were on the north side of this gateway, over the porter's lodge.

The college consists of five courts and the building is called Bishop's Hostel. These courts are known as the Old, or Great Court, Neville's, or Cloister Court, King's, or the New Court, and two courts on the opposite side of the street, to the east of the entrance gateway, called the Whewell Courts. It would be impossible to enter into a description of these beautiful open spaces. They must certainly be seen to be appreciated.

The chapel, which has lately undergone very extensive alterations and improvements, was planned by Henry VIII. It was commenced in 1556 by his daughter Mary, and completed by Elizabeth in or about 1564. It is a spacious edifice of the plain perpendicular-gothic style. Internally it is 204 feet in length, 34 in breadth and 44 in height. At the west end is a fine statue of Sir Isaac Newton, which was presented to the college in 1755, and is considered one of the finest mod-

King's Gateway, Entrance to Trinity College, Cambridge, England.

ern statues in England. The philosopher is represented as standing on a pedestal in a Master of Arts gown with a prism in his hand. This statue when first finished had the mouth closed. A friend pointed this out to the sculptor as a defect, and before morning he had opened the mouth and made it what it is—simply perfection.

In the chapels of all the colleges the master and vice-master have seats on either side of the entrance to the choir; fellows are seated in seats which are continuous with these last, while the scholars and sizars occupy the range of raised seats below the fellows. The rest of the students find their places on benches parallel to the length of the chapel. Each college has a lodge with a porter, who is only too anxious to show visitors around for a small fee of sixpence or a shilling.

Christ's College is the largest in Cambridge. The institution of this college came about in this way: This was formerly the grammar college of God's House, and was originally founded and endowed on a site near to Clare Hall, by William Byngham, rector of St. John Zachary, London, about 1439. At the special request of Henry VI. this house and grounds were given up to him and enlarged for the site of King's College. On the 18th of June, 1446, the king granted Byngham a new charter, with permission to build another house in Preacher's Ward. This house could not have been considered very prosperous, for the revenues were never sufficient for the maintenance of more persons than a proctor or master and four scholars. On the 1st of May, 1505, the Lady Margaret obtained a license from her son, Henry VIII., to change its name to Christ's College, and to endow it for a master, twelve fellows, and forty-seven scholars.

The principal entrance is by a low tower gateway, built entirely of stone. The carved work is very rich and elaborate. It consists of the Lady Margaret's arms, supporters and badges, crowned roses and portcullises, and numerous groups of daisies and marguerites. Through this gateway we are conducted into the first court, which contains the chapel, master's lodge, the hall, which was rebuilt a few years ago, and, on the west side, the library, next to the entrance gateway. At the southeast corner is the entrance to the second or Tree Court. The range of buildings on the right was erected in 1822, while on the east there is a handsome edifice of stone, built in 1642, extending the length of 150 feet.

General View of Oxford, England.

The chapel which is handsome and well-proportioned, is fifty-seven feet long by twenty-seven feet broad. It was finished about the end of 1511, but retains few of its original features, as very expensive alterations were carried out in 1701 and 1702. Over the altar is a painting of the "Descent from the Cross."

There is a library which contains about 13,000 volumes, among which may be enumerated the earlier editions of Milton's "Paradise Lost," a copy of the second edition of Erasmus' Greek Testament, printed on vellum at Basle in 1519.

The master's lodge is small in comparison with those of other colleges. It is situated between the hall and chapel and contains a fine portrait of Dr. Covell.

While taking a stroll, the Captain, as was his custom, stopped one day to interview a native, and ask him certain questions, not forgetting to let him know that he was an American.

"I would like to go to your country," remarked the native.

"Yes," replied the Captain, "and you would never forget it. We have the greatest country on earth."

"But don't the insurrectionists cause you trouble?" was the reply.

"The insurrectionists; what do you mean by that?"

"Why, the Indians from Massachusetts."

The Captain could not reply. He first gazed on the native, then at me, and as we left him and passed on, the Captain remarked:

"I wonder if all the world is made up of such idiots?"

St. John's College is a fine old establishment, the front entrance built after the style of an ancient castle. It derives its name from the hospital dedicated to St. John the Evangelist. It is said to have been founded as early as 1135, by Henry Frost. In 1505, Lady Margaret Beaufort, Countess of Richmond and Derby, and mother of King Henry VII., took measures for converting the aforesaid hospital into a college for secular scholars. Various causes having prevented this from being effected during her lifetime, she had it added as a codicil to her will, empowering the executors to carry out her design. The countess died on June 29, 1509, and on Jan. 20, 1510, the hospital was dissolved. On the 9th of April following her executors established on the site thereof the present college. Entering the gateway, we come to the first court, and at the right corner is the new chapel belonging to this college. It is one of the finest churches in Cam-

King's College, Cambridge, England.

bridge, built of Ancaster stone and in the style of architecture which prevailed about 1280, commonly called "Early Decorated." The extreme length of the chapel is 193 feet, and the breadth 52 feet, while the ante-chapel is 89 feet. The height is 50 feet to the top of the parapet, and to the ridge of the roof, 80 feet. There are some very fine wood carvings as well as stained glass windows in this chapel, that must be seen to be appreciated.

In 1326 Clare College was founded, under the style of Clare Hall. It is delightfully situated on the eastern bank of the Cam, and consists of one spacious court, which is entered by two highly ornamented porticos. The court is handsomely built throughout with stone and presents the most uniformly finished appearance of any college in the University.

One of the most imposing buildings in Cambridge is the Fitz-Williams Museum. The University is indebted to the munificence of one of its own members, Richard, Viscount Fitz-Williams, M. A., of Trinity Hall, who died Feb. 5, 1816, and bequeathed to the University his paintings, drawings, prints, books and works of art, together with $500,000 in South Sea stock, the dividends of which were to be expended in the erection of a museum for the reception of his whole collection. The site was purchased of St. Peter's for the sum of about $50,000, and this magnificent building was erected. It was commenced in 1837 and completed about 1848. During the erection of the building, the architect, George Basevi, fell from a scaffold on the Ely Cathedral and was killed. It is estimated the cost of the entire property, as it now stands, is about $500,000. The building contains a vast collection of pictures and other curiosities that cannot help interesting the visitor.

The University Library dates back to about 1424. The front of the library is a fairly handsome building in the Italian style of architecture. Here are shelved about 400,000 volumes of printed books and about 3000 manuscripts, of almost every age and language.

The Observatory was erected in 1822-24, at an expense of about $90,000; $30,000 of this was contributed by subscription and the balance was granted from the University. It is equipped with all that is modern in the way of telescopes, lenses, etc.

I am just reminded here that during the Queen's great Diamond Jubilee procession, when all the royalty and the notables were passing,

New College, Cloister and Tower, Oxford, England.

the Captain called my attention to a carriage filled with ladies in elegant costumes, and then referred to his program.

"There," said the Captain, "that beats anything I ever saw!"

I asked him what he referred to.

"Why," he said, "that carriage contains the Ladies of the Bed Chamber. Did you ever see a lot of servants dressed in such style as they are?"

"About the year of our Lord, 727, lived in the city of Oxford a prince named Didan." So Antony Wood begins his charming story of St. Frideswyde, the daughter of Didan, and, continuing, he says: "Her father built here a church, as the lady, with doubtful saintship, utterly disliked the notion that she should, being a princess, be subject to her inferiors.

"After this Frideswyde took the veil in her own nunnery, but she was not allowed to rest in peace for, 'being accounted the flower of all these parts,' she was sought in marriage of Algar, King of Leicester. This 'young and sprightly prince' would not take a refusal, and even when his ambassadors were smitten with blindness for treacherously endeavoring to carry off the lady, he himself, 'breathing out fire and sword intended for Oxen.' Frideswyde took refuge in a shelter for swine among the woods at Bampton, but Algar still pursued her, till he too was smitten with blindness. She, however, did not return to Oxford for three years, and when she did return at last, the citizens 'lived,' if I might say, 'in a golden age,' no king or enemy durst approach Oxford. She died in 739 and was buried in her own church, of which a fragment may perhaps be seen."

Of this story, mixed as it is with legend, much appears to be true, and around the shrine of St. Frideswyde grew up Oxford. It was a town of importance long before it was the home of the University. Apart from the story of St. Frideswyde, the earliest mention of Oxford is in 912, when the great "King Edward took Lundenbyrg and Oxnaford and all the lands adjacent thereto."

This conjunction of Oxford with London shows its importance. The history of the town is an interesting one during the past six hundred years. It is an elegant city and by many said to far surpass that of Cambridge, although, personally, I was more impressed with my visit to Cambridge than at Oxford. There are located here twenty-one colleges. The style of architecture of the buildings is very similar to those at Cambridge, while the University is managed in a similar manner, each college being practically separate, but all under the charge of one head.

It was at this stage of our visit to Oxford that I asked the Captain how he was pleased with what he had seen.

"I am not pleased at all," was his gruff reply.

In astonishment I asked him what there was that had disappointed him.

"Why," he answered, "before we came here you told me we were going to see the 'Great Seat of Learning,' and we have been through all these buildings and I have not seen the seat yet."

Just then my attention was attracted by an organ grinder who was playing the "Bonnie Blue Flag," and as "music hath charms to soothe the savage breast," I controlled myself with the desired effect.

New College is one of the finest in the city. This was founded on June 30, 1379, by William of Wykeham, Bishop of Winchester, and was built on a plot of ground in the northeast angle of the city, the fortified wall being its boundary and defense. It was opened with solemn religious ceremonial April 14, 1386, and after the lapse of five hundred years most of the buildings remain to this day as they were designed by the munificent founder. In connection with this college is a fine old cloister and a chapel that are very interesting.

The Magdalen College was founded in 1458 by William Patten, and built in 1475-81. The entrance to the college is through a new porter's lodge, adjoining the new entrance gate, in what is called the Old Quadrangle of St. John Baptist. The chapel is in the southeast corner of the quadrangle, from which was formerly delivered annually a sermon on St. John the Baptist's Day to a congregation assembled in front of the same, the ground being strewn with rushes and grass and the building adorned with green boughs in commemoration of the preaching of the Baptist in the wilderness. This custom fell into disuse about 1750, but it survived in the University sermon in the college chapel, annually, on the 24th of June, until last year, 1896, when the sermon was preached from the old pulpit. Each chapel is entered under the Muniment Tower by a door to the right. This was completed in 1840, and is very interesting. The altar-piece, "Christ Bearing His Cross," is ascribed to Ribalta, a Spaniard.

Corpus Christi College was founded in 1516 by Richard Fox, Bishop of Winchester and Keeper of the Privy Seal of Henry VII.

and Henry VIII. Bishop Fox's original design was to erect a seminary for eight monks of St. Swithun's Priory, in Winchester, with a few secular scholars, but this plan was altered, it is said, at the suggestion of the Bishop of Exeter, who remonstrated thus:

"What, my lord, shall we build houses and provide livelihoods for a company of buzzing monks, whose end and fall we, ourselves, may live to see? No, no; it is more meet, a great deal, that we should care to provide for the increase of learning, and for such as, by their learning, shall do good in the church and commonwealth."

Entering by the tower gateway, with fine vaulted roof, is the hall, which possesses good timber roof of the sixteenth century, and contains portraits of benefactors. On its summit are carved the arms of Henry VII. Several objects of antiquarian interest are treasured as relics of this college. Among them is the pastoral staff, in perfect preservation, though nearly four hundred years old. There is also an original portrait of Bishop Fox, executed by Fleming, early in the reign of Henry VIII.

Pembroke College was endowed by Thomas Tesdale and Richard Wightwick, named after William, Earl of Pembroke, then the Chancellor of the University. Almost all the present buildings of Pembroke College are quite modern, the chapel being a fair specimen of the heavy classic of the Georgian period, and was begun in 1728, the year of Dr. Johnson's entrance into the college, and was consecrated in 1732. Adjoining Pembroke College, with its east front facing Christ's Church, is the house originally founded by Cardinal Wolsey, though not completed until 1834. There is a very fine picture gallery in Oxford, which contains a fine series of portraits of university benefactors and other interesting pictures.

In addition to this is the Bodleian Library. The most ancient portion of this Library, over the Divinity School, was founded by Humphrey, Duke of Gloucester, son of Henry IV., in 1455-80. When one enters he is struck by the stillness and solemnity that reigns around, helped by the dimly lighted windows with painted glass, ponderous shelves, the illuminated missals and the graduates and attendants conversing in low whispers as they move quietly around. Bodleian Library contains over half a million volumes and manuscripts, and other rich literary treasures. The University Museum was built and opened in 1860. It contains a fine collection of interesting relics.

Entrance to Wadham College, Oxford, England.

Probably the most interesting building in Oxford is the Sheldonean Theatre, where the college commencements usually take place, where students compete in English and other courses for prizes offered by the Faculty. The Sheldonean Theatre is a circular building, the floor being used on state occasions for the scholars and the first gallery for the spectators. It is a most interesting building to visitors.

Another view of Oxford can be obtained from the cupola on the roof. There are many other fine colleges and places of interest in Oxford, but space will not permit of any further description of the same.

While we were preparing to leave Oxford, the Captain asked me where we were next bound for.

"Windsor," I replied, "the most famous place in England."

"You are right," said the Captain. "I suppose there is more soap manufactured there than in any other town in the world."

"Soap," I answered; "what do you mean by that?'

"Why, 'Old Brown Windsor Soap,'" returned the Captain. "Isn't that what the place is famous for?"

Who will disagree with me when I say there are times in a man's life when he is justified in doing desperate things?

CHAPTER XVI.

Windsor Castle and Eton College.

"THERE is no place in Great Britain I want to visit more than I do Windsor Castle," remarked the Captain to me on our journey there. I supposed, of course, the Captain was interested in its historic attractions, and paid no further attention to his remark until our arrival at our destination, when, meeting one of the policemen on guard, he inquired :

"In which apartments does the Queen reside?"

The policeman pointed out the apartments occupied by Her Majesty when in residence here.

"Now," said the Captain, addressing me, "is the moment I have looked forward to for many years."

"How so?" I asked.

"Why, an introduction to the Queen," was the reply.

"An introduction to the Queen!" I answered. "What do you mean?"

"Why," said the Captain, "the old lady lives here, and it is my intention to have an introduction to her before I depart."

And then I went out and, contrary to my custom, drank a quart of "'alf an' 'alf" to drown my sorrow.

Probably there is no place outside of London of more interest to the tourist than Windsor Castle. Windsor is about 22 miles distant from London, and about 40 minutes by rail. A very pleasant journey can be made there by taking the boat on the Thames and going as far as Henley, stopping over night, and thence by boat to Windsor the next morning. Windsor is a spot favored by nature with the richest and most variegated scenery, diversified by hill and dale, beautiful parks, luxuriant forests and verdant meadows, and animated by the windings of a noble river, selected for the residence of the sovereigns of England, and enjoying for centuries the presence and support of an elegant court, together with its historical associations and events, and the magnificent works of art by which the stately castle is adorned. I think that the traveler who has toured Europe and come back to Windsor will agree with me that this is the most elegant castle on the other side of the great ocean.

The first authentic notice of Windsor, called by the Saxons, "Windleshore," from the winding course of the River Thames in the vicinity, appears from a donation which King Edward the Confessor made thereof to the monks of Westminster, wherein it is declared that the king, " for the hope of eternal reward and the remission of all sins, the sins of his father, mother and all of his ancestors, to the praise of the Almighty God, grants Windleshore with all its appurtenances, as an endowment and perpetual inheritance to the monks that there serve God." The monks however, were not long permitted to retain the gift, for William the Conqueror, in the first year of his reign, 1066, being struck by the beauty of the neighborhood, the salubrity of the air, its convenience to the pleasures of the chase and its vicinity to woods and waters, selected it as a residence. He therefore required the monks to resign it into his possession and accept in exchange certain lands and estates in the County of Essex. The king forthwith built a castle upon the hill, containing fifty acres. The castle in Henry III.'s time occupied the space now called lower ward. The hall of the palace is now used as the Deans' and Canons' Library. It is impossible to trace the form of the castle previous to Edward III. The magnificent improvements which the castle underwent in his reign were, no doubt, due to the affection which Edward bore to his native place.

While we were strolling though the grounds of Windsor Castle, I was telling the Captain something of its early history, and asked him if it was not romantic.

"I don't see anything romantic in it," was his reply. "To tell you the truth, all the time you have been talking I have been thinking you have a swelled head."

"Why so?" I asked.

"Oh! all this bosh about William the Conquerer, Edward the Confessor, and I don't know what," he replied, "you are getting too English."

I assured the Captain I did not understand him, and that while I admired what we had seen and were seeing, yet I was as true a patriot to my own country as he was.

Windsor Castle, East Terrace.

"Well," he returned, "if that is the case, give us a rest, and show me a picture of George the Third as he looked when he heard our Declaration of Independence."

I told him Kodaks were not invented then, and he appeared satisfied.

New Windsor is situated on the eastern border of the County of Berkshire and has always had the designation of New to distinguish it from Old Windsor, a pleasant village about two miles distant. The castle is located directly opposite the station, about three minutes' walk, and is built on the summit of a hill, about one hundred feet above the level of the Thames; and here was the home of the rulers of Great Britain: William the Conqueror; Henry I., who celebrated here in great state his marriage with his queen, Adelais of Lorraine; King Henry II., who held a parliament in the castle in 1170, and during the contest between King John and the barons, which terminated in the granting of Magna Charta, the former took refuge in the castle which in the year subsequent to the signing of the Charter was ineffectually besieged by the barons. During the reign of Henry III. the castle was alternately in possession of both the contending factions. Edward I. and Edward II. made Windsor their principal residence. It is likewise the birthplace of several of their children, the most celebrated of whom was Edward III., who rebuilt it with the exception of three towers at the west end of the lower ward. The celebrated William of Wykeham superintended the works at a weekly salary of seven shillings for himself and three shillings per week for his clerk.

Edward IV. rebuilt upon an enlarged scale the chapel of St. George, in which his remains were subsequently deposited, as well as those of his unfortunate rival, Henry VI. Henry VII. made several additions to the chapel and upper ward. The ill-fated Charles I. resided in the castle at the commencement of his reign, and held occasional courts in these apartments, which, towards the close of his eventful career, he was obliged to inhabit as prisoner. Soon after the Restoration Charles II. adopted Windsor Castle as his favorite residence and commenced a series of alterations. William III. and Queen Anne improved the parks, planting several avenues of elm and beech trees. George I. frequently resided at the castle, where every Thursday he dined in public, a fashionable custom at that period

Windsor Castle, Norman Gateway.

in continental courts. With the exception of trifling occasional repairs the ward remains as it was left by Charles II. until the reign of George III., who selected Windsor as his principal residence. In 1284 Parliament granted $1,500,000 towards the improvement of the building the expenditure of which was placed under the superintendence of seven commissioners. Various other sums have since been voted, amounting in the aggregate to more than $4,500,000.

King Henry VIII. Gateway on Castle Hill forms the entrance to the lower ward, which is divided by St. George's Chapel, on the north of which are the residences of the ecclesiastical officers of the establishment, and on the south those of the military knights. The residence of the lay clerks is in what is styled the Horse Shoe Cloisters. The Curfew or Belfry Tower was erected by Henry III. about the twenty-fifth year of his reign.

The Captain was much interested in the last resting place of Sir Henry Wooten, a provost of Eton College, who had the following curious epitaph inscribed about his grave:

> Here lies the author of this sentence
> "An itching for dispute is the scab of the church."
> Seek his name elsewhere.

The Captain gazed at this for a few moments and turning to me remarked :

" I do not know how long that fellow has been dead, but it seems to me any one that was the author of such a sentence as that is a better dead man than he would be a live man. Any rooster that wants to get into a dispute around these diggings should be, in my opinion, *non est*."

The State Apartments are a series of splendid rooms, commanding a beautiful prospect of the surrounding country, with large picture galleries, consisting of the Van Dyke room, with a choice collection of the paintings of this famous artist ; the Zuccarelli room, with some of the specimens of this artist. The state ante chamber, the ceiling of which represents "The Banquet of the Gods," painted by Verrio, also contains several beautiful tapestries. From this we reach the grand staircase, which forms an approach worthy of so splendid an edifice. The grand vestibule is 47 feet long, 28 feet wide and 45 feet high. This contains suits of armor of the time of Elizabeth and Charles I., and here are also displayed Her Majesty's Jubilee presents given her at the golden jubilee in 1887. From this vestibule we enter the Waterloo chamber. This is 45 feet high, 98 feet long and 47 feet wide, and is finished in the style of architecture which flourished in the time of Elizabeth and contains many portraits and paintings in connection with the battle of Waterloo. From here we pass to the throne room, a stately apartment, finished in rich blue, which at once reminds the visitor of the imposing ceremonials which from time to time take place here in the presence of the Sovereign of the Most Noble Order of the Garter. The panels of the room are enriched by paintings. The throne is carved from ivory and is of Indian workmanship. It was first shown at the great exhibition of 1851, and was presented to the Queen by Maharajah Travancore. The grand reception room is next in order and is 90 feet long, 34 feet broad and 33 feet high. It contains a magnificent Gothic window, filled with plate glass and forming almost the entire north end of the room, opening upon a beautiful and extensive prospect over the parks and adjacent country. The general style of the room is necessarily Gothic, to correspond with the exterior of the building, and is that of the time of Louis XIV. The workmanship is admirable, and some very elegant tapestries adorn the wall.

St. George's Hall is next reached and is 200 feet long, 34 feet broad and 32 feet high Entering this room one is struck with its princely dimensions, more than surprised by the extra magnificence. The ceiling is in Gothic style. There are thirteen windows on the south side of the room, and on the opposite are recesses, in which are placed full length portraits of the last eleven sovereigns of England.

In the Music Gallery at the eastern end is a powerful organ, beneath which is the Chair of State, richly carved in steel, similar to the Coronation Chair at Westminster Abbey. The banners and arms of the original companionship of the Knights of the Most Noble Order of the Garter, as founded by King Edward III. in 1344, are hung in this apartment. The Guard Tower is next reached and is 78 feet long, 31 feet high, and contains many interesting objects. Passing on we come to the Queen's Presence Chamber. The ceiling is adorned with a fine painting, by Verrio, of Catherine of Braganza, Queen of Charles II. She is represented as seated under a canopy, spread by Time and supported by zephyrs, while Religion, Prudence and Fortitude and other virtues are in attendance on her. Fame is proclaiming the happiness of the country and Justice is driving away Sedition, Envy and Discord. The walls are wainscoated with oak and decorated with four large and splendid specimens of Gobelin tapestry. We next enter the Queen's Audience Chamber. The ceiling of this apartment is also painted by Verrio, the subject being Queen Catherine of Braganza, Queen of Charles II., personified as Britannia.

The private apartments may occasionally be seen by special permission. These apartments are elegantly furnished and enriched with the most elaborate decorations, containing every requisite and accommodation for the sovereign and her immediate attendants. They are occupied by the Queen when in residence here and contain some very fine paintings, one room especially being given up to Rubens' works.

Between the two wards of the castle is situated the Keep, or Round Tower, which is built on the summit of a lofty artificial mount. This is open to visitors and a sight well worth viewing is to be had from the summit.

A most interesting part of the castle is the Albert Memorial Chapel, and when we take into consideration the comparative smallness of its dimensions, it may be said to have one of the most splendid interiors in the world. Its dimensions are, length sixty-eight feet, breadth twenty-eight feet, and sixty feet high. Without viewing the edifice it is impossible to realize the rich beauty of its magnificent decorations. The interior has been fitted up with great magnificence by Queen Victoria, in memory of the Prince Consort. The entire vaulted roof is covered with mosaic figures, ornaments and inscriptions; the stained glass windows are of surpassing richness and color and very superior workmanship, showing full length portraits in them, representing the ancestors of the Prince Consort. At the east of the building is placed a cenotaph, with the recumbent figure of the Prince in armor, and at his feet his favorite hound, Eos. The cap of the cenotaph is grand antique marble, which bears this inscription : "Albert, the Prince Consort, born Aug. 25, 1819, died Dec. 14, 1861 ; buried in the Royal Mausoleum at Frogmore. 'I have fought the good fight, I have finished my course.' "

At the west end is the sarcophagus of the late Duke of Albany. In the center of the chapel is the sarcophagus of the late Duke of Clarence and Avondale, son of the Prince of Wales, whose untimely death

in January, 1892, cast such a gloom over the nation. This building was erected by Henry VII. as a burial place for himself and successors. Upon his later preference of Westminister Abbey for that purpose, it remained neglected until Cardinal Wolsey obtained a grant of it from Henry VIII. With the same profusion of expense which marked all the public acts of his life, he began to prepare it as a receptacle for his remains, but at the confiscation of his property it reverted to the Crown.

The following royal personages have been interred here: Prince Octavius and Prince Albert, children of George III.; Duchess of Brunswick; Princess Adelaide and Princess Elizabeth, children of the Duke of Clarence; Prince Harold, infant son of the Prince and Princess Christian of Schleswig-Holstein; Victoria Georgiana, infant daughter of Princess Frederica; Princess Amelia; Princess Charlotte; Duke of Kent; William IV.; Princess Augusta; Queen Adelaide; George III.; George V., King of Hanover.

I called the attention of the Captain to the elegant monuments in Albert Memorial and St. George's Chapel. The Captain gazed on them for a few moments, and his answer was this:

"Yes, they are great monuments, but I don't see one that comes up to Bunker Hill."

What else could I do but pass to the outer door and shed a tear?

St. George's Chapel, one of the most interesting parts of Windsor Castle, was erected by order of Edward IV. about the year 1474, and since that time has been endowed largely by succeeding monarchs. The principal entrance is at the west end of the nave, which has been greatly improved by the erection of a grand flight of stone steps, with a handsome carved balustrade, also in stone. On entering the chapel the admiration of the spectator is immediately excited by the grandeur of its architecture, which is in the perpendicular style, extremely light and elegant in proportion, and unrivaled in the richness of its carvings in stone and oak. The stone roof, which was executed in the reign of King Henry VII., is especially remarkable for its beautiful tracery. The armorial bearings of several sovereigns, including Edward the Confessor, Edward III., Henry VI., Edward IV. and Henry VII., and other illustrious knights companions are emblazoned on the ceiling.

The great west window is a fine specimen of stained glass, containing six tiers and compartments, each six feet in height and displaying

Windsor Castle, Round Tower.

seventy-five figures representing Edward the Confessor, Edward IV.
and Henry VII. The glass in this window was collected from various
parts of the chapel in 1774. A number of interesting monuments are
to be found in St. George's Chapel, among which may be mentioned
that of the Duke of Kent, erected by the Queen to the memory of her
illustrious father.

Crossing over the nave to the west end of the north aisle we find
the magnificent statues of Leopold I., late King of the Belgians, placed
here by the Queen, near the noble monument to his first wife. Here
is also buried Princess Charlotte, whose resting place is covered by a
magnificent cenotaph, which was erected by national subscription.
Opposite the north aisle, near the third window, is a monument to
George V., King of Hanover, consisting of a pillared framework of
polished marble. The vault of Henry VIII. and Charles I. are notable. They are located in the centre of the choir, which is near the
eleventh stall of the sovereign's side, where are deposited the remains
of Henry VIII. and his Queen, Lady Jane Seymour, as well as the
remains of Charles I. and an infant daughter of Queen Anne.

Near the altar is a large memorial window to Prince Albert, representing the Resurrection. On the north side of the arch is the original tomb of Edward IV., which contains his name in raised brass
letters, and is placed on a black marble slab, over which are his arms
and crown, supported by cherubim. In the south aisle is a statue to the
late Emperor Frederick of Germany, executed in pure white marble
and representing the emperor in military costume, wearing his various orders, the hands clasped upon the handle of his sword. In the
middle of the aisle is a large flat carved stone, bearing only the inscription "Henry VI." The remains of this monarch were removed
from Chertsey Abbey, where they were first interred, by command of
Henry VII. In the center of the Braye Chapel has been erected a
monument to the late Prince Imperial of France, by command of the
Queen. This monument is sculptured in white marble, with a recumbent figure, representing the Prince in the uniform which he wore in
Africa during the Zulu war, in which he lost his life. There are
many other interesting monuments and windows that will bear the
closest inspection.

The Captain noticed the British flag floating on Windsor Castle
and other parts of this historic building. I observed that he gave

particular attention to this, and that something was coming sooner or later, but it came sooner than I thought.

"See here," said the Captain, "not a single Star Spangled Banner have I seen during my tour today. I have got tired of this kind of business and want to go back to Boston. The sooner we get there the better I shall feel."

And the Captain pulled out one of his shilling cigars, and I noticed that he lighted the wrong end, smoking away furiously as he mounted the carriage to be driven to Eton College.

Leaving Windsor and ten minutes' walk crossing the Thames, brings one to that venerable and illustrious seminary known as Eton College, which for four centuries has planted the seeds of learning in the expanding mind of youth. This historical institution was founded by King Henry VI. in September, 1440. The buildings were commenced in the following year and when completed contained accommodations for "twenty-five poor grammar scholars and twenty-five poor and infirm men to pray for the king." The present establishment consists of a provost, vice-provost, fifteen fellows, a head master, a lower master, assistants, seventy scholars, seven lay clerks and ten choristers, beside the inferior officers of the collegers. The scholars on the foundation are called collegers, and are distinguished by wearing a black cloth gown. The others are termed oppidans, the expense of whose education and maintenance is defrayed by relatives, and who board in private houses within the precincts of the college. The school is yearly increasing and now numbers about 1000 students. Upon the day of election the senior scholars deliver public orations in the upper school, selected from the classics and best English authors.

The buildings of the college form two large quadrangles and with the exception of the chapel are built of brick, having the roof battlemented. The principal front faces the Thames and a neatly disposed garden extends to the bank of the river. The outer quadrangle is formed on the east side by the clock tower and apartments of some of the masters and on the north by the lower school, above which was formerly a long chamber or dormitory for the scholars on the foundation; on the south side by the chapel, and on the west by the upper school, which, with the stone arcade beneath it, was built by Sir Christopher Wren, at the expense of Dr. Allestre, provost of the college, after the restoration. This room extends the entire width of the college and is adorned with marble busts of King George III William IV., Queen Victoria, Prince Albert, Duke of Wellington, Marquis of Wellesley, Earls of Chatham, Howe and Grey and many other notables. From this place have issued some of the greatest English statesmen, divines, philosophers and poets. In the center of the courtyard is a bronze statue of Henry VI.

The Chapel is a very handsome gothic structure, supported on each side by massive buttresses. It is 175 feet in length, including the ante-chapel at the west end, and has undergone very many improvements since first erected. The ante-chapel is also quite interesting to the observer.

The young gentlemen educated at Eton are greatly addicted to aquatic amusements, and on the fourth of June of each year, in commemoration of the birthday of George III., they go in procession, habited in fancy dresses, in several long boats ornamented with flags and accompanied with music, to a meadow opposite Surly Hall, about three miles up the river, where a collation is provided. On their return a brilliant display of fireworks is exhibited on an island a short distance below Windsor Bridge. The spectacle has been frequently graced with the presence of several members of the royal family, and annually attracts a considerable number of distinguished visitors.

"What do you think of Eton College?" I asked of the Captain after we had finished our inspection of that institution. The Captain was quiet for a few moments evidently in sober thought. His answer came at last:

"The college is all right, I suppose, but I will be hanged if I understand all this royalty business. I haven't seen a single shoe factory in the town."

CHAPTER XVII.

Stoke Poges and Hampton Court.

WHILE journeying from Windsor to Stoke Poges, the Captain was much interested in a description of this historical spot, as related to us by the conductor who had charge of the brake in which we were riding. After describing Stoke Poges and the Poet Gray, the Captain, who had been listening attentively, turned to the conductor and remarked :

"Is old man Gray still living? Does he live at Stoke Poges?"

And to keep the matter quiet I bribed the conductor with two shillings.

Leaving Eton, we pass through a beautiful country on our way to Stoke Poges, the Country Churchyard, and the scene of Gray's "Elegy." What school boy of the present day has not read these lines :

> "The curfew tolls the knell of parting day,
> The lowing herd winds slowly o'er the lea,
> The ploughman homeward plods his weary way,
> And leaves the world to darkness and to me.
>
> "Now fades the glimmering landscape on the sight,
> And all the air a solemn stillness holds,
> Save where the beetle wheels his droning flight,
> And drowsy tinklings lull the distant folds."

Stoke Poges is one of the most interesting spots in England, and a short story of the life of Thomas Gray, the poet, may be appropriate at this point.

Interesting to the students of English country life is the history of any English village, but some spots there are round which lingers the memory of some departed genius, whose spirit seems even after death to hover round the haunts he loved in life, calling men and women from all lands to visit the calm retreat made famous by this muse. Had Shakespeare not lived, Stratford-atte-Bowe would have been as well known as Stratford-upon-Avon ; and but for Gray, Stoke

Church and Churchyard, Stoke Poges, England.

In this churchyard, to the left and under the large tree by the side of the church, is the spot where Thomas Gray wrote his "Elegy." Gray is buried here, his remains resting under the first monument to the left, directly in front of the church.

Poges would have been a name unknown to the world at large. Born at his father's house in Cornhill, on December 26, 1716, Thomas Gray was the only one of a family of twelve who reached maturity. His father was a clever man of business, with extravagant habits and cruel to a degree both to his wife and son. His mother (Dorothy Antrobus, her maiden name) possessed the good sense and kindly heart her husband lacked and seems to have fully deserved the affection her son ever showed her. About 1727, Gray was sent to Eton at his mother's charges, and there begun his famous friendship with Horace Walpole and Richard West. There, too, he gained that love for the literature of Greece and Rome which makes its influence felt in almost every line of his poetry. At Eton, he chose the student's life—"Gray never was a boy," says Walpole—and that choice he never deserted. Pembroke Hall, Cambridge, was his home for a short time in 1734, but he soon left it for Peterhouse, Walpole going to King's a little later, and West to Christ's Church, Oxford. His vacations he spent at his uncle's house at Burnham, where he revelled in the beeches and doubtless found time to explore Stoke Poges. He left Cambridge in 1738, and six months afterwards started on his famous continental tour with Horace Walpole. They began their travels on terms of closest friendship, but two years and a half of close companionship gave birth to differences which parted them in 1741, to come together again in three years' time into a renewal of intimacy only broken by death. In November, 1741, Gray's father died, having before his death succeeded in squandering all his possessions. Mrs. Gray wound up her business in Cornhill and came to live with her sister, Mrs. Rogers, at the farmhouse in Stoke Poges, where Stoke Court now stands. Here, in June, 1742—the month and year that West ("Favonius") died—Gray made his first of many visits to Stoke Poges. At that time the old manor house still stood in its original shape as built in 1555 by the Earl of Huntingdon, and was occupied by Viscount Cobham. Mrs. Rogers' house, where Gray stayed with his mother, was at West End, some three-quarters of a mile from the church which Gray afterwards made so famous. In those days it was a two-story farmhouse, of which the stone fireplace with "1.6.4.8" engraved on it, Gray's bedroom, and the window at which he sat, alone remain in their original condition.

West Front, Wolsey Palace; Hampton Court, England.

There is a fee attached to about every place that one visits in England. As we passed into the yard at Stoke Poges and entered the lodge, we were requested to register and deposit sixpence each.

"What is that for?" asked the Captain.

"Why," I replied, "it is your admission to the graveyard."

"Well," said the Captain eyeing me, "I will be hanged if this isn't the cheapest entrance to a graveyard I ever heard of in my life!"

And if the matron in charge had not stopped him, the Captain would have filled up his pipe and smoked it on the spot.

On a slope some little distance from the house there exists the arbor in which Gray "used to sit and dream," and the scene around is still as calm and remote from all the busy stir of life as when Gray described himself as "still at Stoke, hearing, seeing, doing absolutely nothing." It was in this year, however, that he laid the foundations of his fame. "Exegi monumentem aere perennius" might have been said by Gray if he could have looked into the secrets of the future, for it was in November, 1742, that he began the "Elegy." In August he had written his "Ode to Spring"—famous for "a solitary fly"—an ode that sounded the note of revolt against the dominion of the couplet, a sonnet to the memory of West, his "Ode on a Distant Prospect of Eton College," and the "Ode on Adversity."

In October or November, brooding, perhaps, over the late death of his friend West, and inspired by the quiet rusticity of his surroundings, he began the poem, which more than all others has made his name famous. His uncle, Jonathan Rogers, died at Stoke Poges, on Oct. 31, 1742, and was buried in the neighboring parish of Burnham. There seems to be little doubt that it was very soon after that date that Gray began the composition of the "Elegy," though it was not actually finished till the year 1750. Some jealous souls would try to prove that "the country churchyard" is not that of Stoke Poges. It is enough to remember that Gray began the "Elegy" when residing at Stoke Poges, that for many years he spent his vacations at Stoke Poges, that his aunt and his mother were both buried at Stoke Poges, and that if he knew any country churchyard well that was the one.

It was in 1750, some months after his aunt's burial at Stoke, that he wrote to Walpole: "I have been here at Stoke a few days, having put an end to a thing whose beginning you have seen long ago; I immediately send it to you." Its beginning was at Stoke, at Stoke were added the final touches, and the "weary ploughman's" descendants still plough the Stoke furrows, and in the tower the "moping owl" still rears its brood. There may be some doubt as to the real birthplace of Homer, but none to the country churchyard in which the "Elegy" was "wrote." From this year (the year 1742) begins the second period of Gray's life. Forced by circumstances and the want of money to give up his original idea of reading for the bar, he decided to live at Cambridge, spending all his spare time with his mother and aunt at Stoke. He returned to Peterhouse, and devoted all his hours to study. He deserted his muse and for five years read Greek and little else. In 1747, at Walpole's persuasion, he published his "Ode on a Distant Prospect of Eton College," but it met with scant appreciation. In 1747, also, he immortalized Walpole's cat in a poem that was "rather too long for an epitaph but not too long to delight the lovers of happy trifles." In 1749 his aunt died and was buried at Stoke and shortly afterwards he finished the "Elegy." Walpole received a copy and showed it to his friends and among others to Lady Cobham (then living at the manor house), who had little idea till she was told by the Rev. Robert Purt, that "a wicked imp they called a poet" had been for some years living in her parish. Feminine curiosity was aroused and two messengers of Fate, in the shape of Lady Schaub and Miss Speed (Lady Cobham's niece), invaded the shy poet's retreat, only to find him out. A note was left, the fish rose to the fly, and thus began Gray's intimacy with Lady Cobham, and literature was enriched by a story not too long. The "Long Story," redolent of quiet humor, was written in August, 1750, but not published (except privately) during Gray's lifetime. The "Elegy" was published by Dodsley in 1751, and rapidly went through fifteen editions, meeting with appreciation everywhere. Criticism of such a poem would be here out of place, but what was written of it by Dr. Johnson, who had a very poor opinion of Gray's merits as a poet, is interesting: "It abounds with images which find a mirror in every mind, and with sentiments to which every bosom returns an echo. The four stanzas beginning, 'Yet ev'n these bones,' are to me original. I have never seen the notions in any other place. Yet he that reads them here persuades himself that he has always felt them.

Had Gray written often thus it had been vain to blame and useless to praise him."

After we had strolled over some of the most interesting parts of the church at Stoke Poges and the grounds surrounding it, the Captain in the meantime giving close attention to the description related by our attendant, he turned to me and whispered.

"Who was this fellow Gray?"

"Why," I replied, "he was a celebrated poet of his time, nearly two hundred years ago, and he was the author of 'Gray's Elegy,' famous as one of the greatest productions from the pen of man."

"You say he was a poet," replied the Captain.

"Certainly," I answered. "A famous poet."

"Then," said the Captain, as he broke off a twig from near his tomb, "he is the chap that wrote 'Beautiful Snow,' isn't he?"

And the Captain glanced skyward and said it looked like rain, while I almost hoped it might be a deluge.

The year 1753 saw the first appearance of a collection of Gray's poems in the shape of the "Six Poems, by T. Gray," published by R. Bentley, and containing a portrait of the poet. The same year Mrs. Gray died, and was buried at Stoke, he, her son composing the epitaph, which may still be read: "In the same pious confidence, beside her friend and sister, here sleep the remains of Dorothy Gray, widow, the careful mother of many children, one of whom alone had the misfortune to survive her." His mother's death left Gray with a sufficient competence to enable him to live on at Cambridge in the simple fashion he loved best; and, except for occasional visits to friends and tours to Scotland and the Lakes, and a three years' stay in London, the rest of his life was spent in that town.

In 1754 he wrote the "Progress of Poesy," which quickly brought him to the front as a master of English lyrics, and the following year he began "The Bard." A silly freak of some undergraduates at Peterhouse, who knew of Gray's constitutional terror of fire, led him to leave his rooms at that college and accept the welcome willingly offered him at Pembroke, where for the last fifteen years of his life he spent his time quietly and happily among his books and his flowers. Some concerts given at Cambridge by John Parry, the famous blind harper, set "all his learned body a dancing," and spurred him on to the completion of "The Bard." There was no

The Great Hall, Hampton Court, England.

living poet who approached him either in the estimation of the public or of the literary world ; and on Colley Cibber's death, in 1757, he was offered the post of poet laureate. Partly from a disinclination to be "at war with the little fry of his own profession," he thought fit to decline. In 1758 his aunt, Mrs. Rogers, died at Stoke, and Gray shut up West End Farm, only visiting the village rarely during the rest of his life. The next three years he spent in London, living in Southampton row, close to the British Museum, then in its infancy, but even in its earliest days a real treasure to a student such as Gray. It was at this time that some friends of his thought, and perhaps hoped that he would marry Lady Cobham's neice, Miss Speed. He confined himself, however, to writing her a sonnet, which has but little of the ring of a successful wooer, and gave himself up to his books and his friends.

In 1762 the post of professor of modern history and modern languages at Cambridge fell vacant, and Gray's friends tried, but in vain, to secure his election. Other influences were more powerful, and it was not until 1768 that he was elected to the only post he ever seems to have coveted. During the next few years he took great interest in Icelandic literature, and the "Descent of Odin" and the "Fatal Sisters," show what time he must have bestowed upon his study of a new and difficult language. Few events ruffled the tenor of his last years. Travels in the South, travels in the north of England, an occasional visit to Mason at York, and a short tour in the Highlands occupied his vacations, while his time at Cambridge slipped happily along, cheered by his friendship with Nichols and Bonstetten, whose frankness, gaiety and love of literature did much to enliven Gray's last two years.

For some time his health had been poor, and a visit to London in May, 1771, did him little good. Troubled with gout, neuralgia and an incessant cough, he went back to Cambridge in July, after paying his last visit to Walpole. On July 24 he was taken seriously ill while at dinner in a hall at Pembroke, and after five days' illness he passed quietly away, comforted at the end by the presence of Mary Antrobus, his niece. On August 5 he was, according to his own desire, buried in the churchyard he loved, "in the vault made by my late dear mother." And there he lies, with only a simple stone on the church wall opposite to mark the place. Erected by John Penn there is a monument, only interesting through the verses inscribed upon it ;

and the best memorial to Gray is the spirit which yearly brings hundreds of visitors to gaze upon his tomb.

Here at Stoke Poges was the home of William Penn, the founder of Pennsylvania. His ancestors are buried in the country churchyard, and there have been erected here several tablets to their memory.

No more delightful trip can be taken from London than a visit to Hampton Court. A pleasant way to reach this spot is a boat ride on the Thames to Hampton and return on the top of a 'bus through Bushy woods to Richmond, where a change is made for a tram car, which will convey the tourist to Kew, thence, on top of a 'bus, into London, passing through a delightful country with most beautiful scenery.

After our visit at Stoke Poges, the Captain and myself stood in a neighboring field surveying the beautiful rustic scenery that lay before us, when I asked him how he was impressed with his visit here.

"Well," replied the Captain, "I suppose you like it. I did not come to England to visit old graveyards, and the next best thing to do is to find out if there is a good continuous show around. If there is we will take that in."

Hampton Court was originally built by Cardinal Wolsey, who presented it to his sovereign, Henry VIII. It was the birthplace of Edward VI; the masques and tournaments of Phillip, Mary and Elizabeth occurred here; also the celebration of the marriage of Cromwell's daughter to Lord Falconbury. The palace is a splendid structure of red brick with stone ornaments and is almost entirely devoted at the present time to an exhibition of pictures. There are portraits of many of the great beauties of Charles II.'s Court, besides other paintings of many of the old masters, among them a fine picture of Charles II. on horseback, by Van Dyck. The entrance to the palace is through the gates at the foot of Hampton Court Bridge. Historic associations, awakened by the many very opposite aspects of the place, will then arise in chronological review, and the numerous beauties will reach their climax, as one makes his exit from the gardens.

Entering the gateway, one passes along to what is known as the first courtyard of Wolsey's palace, which is indeed grand and worthy of description. Just before entering the courtyard and turning to the left, passing up a broad flight of stairs, the visitor enters what is known as the great hall, which formed no part of the original palace, but was not commenced until five years after the Cardinal had given up Hampton Court to Henry VIII. The main attraction of these halls are the elegant glass windows representing a variety of historical incidents, among which is the pedigree of the six wives of Henry VIII; also the fine tapestries with which the walls are hung, and which are some of the oldest in Europe.

As noted above, Henry VIII. added much to Hampton Court after receiving it as a gift from Wolsey. Anne Boleyn went hence to be beheaded, Jane Seymour came hither to give birth to Edward VI., after which she died; Philip and Mary passed a gloomy honeymoon here; James I. held here in 1604 his conferences with the bishops and Puritan leaders. He talked much Latin and disputed with Dr. Reynolds, telling the petitioners that they wanted to strip Christ again, and bade them get away with their snivelling. When they besought leave to hold their prophesying meetings, he cried out violently: "Ay, is it that ye would be at? If you aim at a Scotch Presbytery, let me tell you, it agrees as well with monarchy as God and the devil; then shall Jack and Tom and Will and Dick meet, and censure my council; therefore, I reiterate my former speech—'*Le roi s'avisera.*' Stay, I pray you, for one seven years, before you demand, and then if you grow pursy and fat, I may perchance hearken to you, for that government will keep me in health, and find me work enough." The end of it was, that he cried out, "No bishop, no king!"

"Well Captain," I remarked, as we were enjoying the sights in and around the grand old palace, "one can hardly realize that this was once the stronghold of Cardinal Wolsey."

"How do you know it was?" he replied.

"It's a matter of history," I added.

"History be hanged!" said the Captain as he faced me. "What had Wolsey to do with history?"

"What had Wolsey to do with history?" I returned, "why he was the man that at one time controlled the destiny of England."

"Go tell that to the marines," shouted the Captain. "The only man who ever controlled the destiny of England, was George Washington."

And the Captain left me and went to examine an old piece of tapestry and asked the attendant if it was "sold by the yard or by the piece."

Charles I. escaped from Hampton Court in 1647, only to be placed in stricter confinement in Carisbrooke Castle. Oliver Cromwell

Entrance to Pond Garden, Hampton Court, England.

made Hampton Court his residence and probably was the means of arresting its sale. Charles II. gave the palace to the Duke of Albermarle, who afterwards redeemed it and occupied it himself. William and Mary were the founders of the modern parts. An interesting feature of the palace is the astronomical clock over the gateway in the second quadrangle. A few paces to the southeast corner, across the clock court, takes us into the Ionic colonnade of Sir Christopher Wren, beautiful in itself, but very much misplaced here. This colonnade leads to the king's great staircase, which is the best approach to the state rooms. We might fancy ourselves in the palace of Louis XV. instead of that of a British sovereign.

Leaving the great hall and passing over the courtyard, a tour of the apartments of the palace is commenced in what is known as Room No. 1 and continued to No. 32, there being about thirty-two apartments devoted to pictures and a few articles of historic interest. In the great watching chamber is to be found a fine lot of tapestries which were hung here in the time of Wolsey and that manifestly belonged to a period anterior to those in the hall.

In Room No. 6, known as the state bedroom of King William III. will be found the state bed of Queen Charlotte, brought from Windsor. The lilac satin draperies of the bed were embroidered by the Clergy Orphan School for Queen Charlotte, consort of George III. Verrio painted the ceiling, which represents Night and Day. At the head of the bed is a clock made by Daniel Quare, which needs winding only once a year. In Room No. 11, known as Queen Anne's bedroom, is seen the state bed of Queen Anne, with its hangings which were worked at Spitalfields. The ceiling was painted by Sir James Thornhill, and represents Aurora rising out of the sea in her golden chariot, drawn by four white horses and attended by Cupids. Entering Room 12, a magnificent view of the gardens at Hampton Court is to be obtained from the windows. This should not be lost, and is only equaled by a similar view at the Palace of Versailles. Room 19 is known as the Queen's private chapel. It is very small, yet answers the purpose for which it was intended. Queen Caroline was accustomed to have prayers read by her chaplain in a room adjoining her private chamber, while she was dressing. Her toilet was performed in the little room next to this, called the Queen's bath closet. In Room No. 21, known as the private dining room, is now placed the state bed of King William III., on the left with crimson damask. On

Anne Boleyn's Gateway, Hampton Court, England.

the right, hung with crimson, is that of his queen, Mary. Some of the lace with which this was formerly covered still remains. There is a small bed in the center of this room that was used by King George II. when he resided at this palace.

In making a tour of the rooms a very fine view of what is known as the Fountain Court can be obtained. Its dimensions are 110x117 feet with a cloister on all four sides.

Leaving the palace, a walk can be taken through the delightful gardens, which now resemble a magnificent park, with wide walks, trees, shrubbery and grass in profusion.

In the rear of the palace is what is known as the vinery, entirely covered with the grapes, growing from the ceilings of the terraces. This is the private property of Queen Victoria, and the grapes are grown here for her table. The grape vines in this vinery are ninety years old, and yield 3000 bunches of grapes a year. It is estimated that there are from 150,000 to 250,000 people visit Hampton Court each year.

While passing out of the gate of the courtyard at Hampton Court, a seedy-looking individual approached the Captain and looking him in the face remarked:

" 'Ow are ye, guv'ner? It is a long time since I've seen ye."

The Captain looked at him and remarked:

"You must be mistaken; I do not know as I ever met you before."

"V'y," said the individual, "don't you remember me? Johnson, the cab driver? It can't be that you have forgotten your old friend, Johnson?"

The Captain straightened up and grasped the man's hand, remarking: "Johnson, is this you? I hadn't the slightest idea of meeting you here in England. What can I do for you?"

"Well, guv'ner," was the reply, "if you can lend me a bob for a couple of days, I will thank you very much."

And without further parley, the Captain passed a shilling over to the beggar, who, bowing, passed on.

After his departure, I asked the Captain why it was he encouraged such people. Turning to me the Captain remarked:

"Wouldn't you do a favor for a friend? That is old Johnson, the cab driver; many a time I have seen him around the Old Colony depot in Boston."

And then I felt worse than I did when I crossed the English Channel.

CHAPTER XVIII.

The Home of Shakespeare.

UPON our arrival at Stratford-on-Avon, the Captain was much interested in the quaint old town and, after looking around for a while, he turned to me and remarked:

"And so this is the home of Shakespeare?"

"Yes," I replied, "this is the home of the historic bard."

"Let me see," said the Captain, and he paused for a moment.

"What are you thinking of?" I asked.

"I was just thinking," said the Captain, "that the old fellow wrote some kind of a play, didn't he?"

"Why, yes," I replied. "He did."

"What I was thinking about," remarked the Captain, "was the name of the play. If I remember rightly it was 'Under the Gaslight.'"

I never in my life felt more like drowning myself.

Among the numerous visitors to Stratford-on-Avon, the birthplace and home of Shakespeare, Americans form the most important contingent. It seems singular, but it is nevertheless the fact that few Britons realize how much they owe to these pilgrims to the old home. Most of the historic objects of the greatest possible value have been spared from destruction because of their popularity with Americans, and many a Briton has been shamed into an interest in the priceless treasures of his own land by the intimate knowledge of such treasures, shown by cultivated Americans.

Stratford is easily reached from London by direct rail through a charming country, a distance of about one hundred miles. There are no large hotels at Stratford, but numerous small and comfortable ones, the chief of which may be mentioned as that of the Red Horse, famous as the stopping place of our own Washington Irving, as well as other well-known Americans.

As the birthplace of Shakespeare it might be apropos to mention here a little of the early history of the family, which dates back to the fifteenth century. John Shakespeare, William's father, was born in 1530, and apprenticed when fourteen years old to a glover in Stratford-on-Avon. The family had been in very poor circumstances up to this time, and in his case he would be free of his apprenticeship in 1551. The town records show that he resided in Henley street in that year, and in 1556 he was described as a glover. In the last year named he bought two houses, one on Henley street and another on Greenhill street, and also sued a neighbor to the value of about eight quarters of barley, from which we may gather he was an active business man. Meanwhile as his business prospered he had doubtless kept well in touch with Robert Arden, his father's landlord, and his own uncle by marriage, as he had succeeded in winning the affections of Mary, the youngest daughter of Robert Arden.

John Shakespeare married in 1557, and on September 5, 1558, John Shakespeare's first child was baptized in the name of Joan at the parish church, and a second daughter, Margaret, was baptized December 2, 1562, and buried on April 30, 1563. On April 26, 1564, was baptized Gulielmus Filius Johannes Shakespeare, otherwise known as William Shakespeare, and as it was usual to baptize a child three days after birth, the 23d of April has been recorded as the birthday of the great poet.

At five years of age he went to the "petty school," and at seven to the grammar school, where he probably remained until he was fourteen. About this time the affairs of the family were under a cloud, business was no longer prosperous and there was probably some ill feeling between John Shakespeare and some of his influential neighbors. It seems unlikely that William remained in school later than fourteen, for his father had need of his help. This, however, is contradicted by other authorities, one especially, that of a recent author, Edward James Castle, Q. C., who suggests from evidence in the plays themselves that Shakespeare began life as a boy actor, playing women's parts. Therefore we can only speculate as to how the time was filled between the poet's schooldays and his eighteenth year, when he married Anne Hathaway, the daughter of a Shottery farmer, his bride being eight years older than the poet. It has been suggested that they lived unhappily, but authorities have not been

House in Which Shakespeare Was Born, Stratford-on-Avon, England.

able to find any evidence to that fact. The scene of the wedding is not exactly known, though the date is approximately fixed by a bond given at Worcester in November, 1582, in connection with the license. The short time elapsing between the date of this bond and the baptism of a daughter in May, 1582, has given rise to the suggestion that the legal marriage had been preceded by a hand-fasting, which was a popular and also perfectly legal, though incomplete, form in those days.

About a week before our departure for home, the Captain was entertaining a party of Englishmen, in the smoking room, with stories of the new world across the sea. During an intermission, one of them turned to him and remarked:

"Well, you may say what you please, but we have the satisfaction of knowing we are five hours ahead of you, and you can never catch up with us."

In England the time is five hours earlier than in the United States, yet this did not disturb my friend, for he immediately, replied:

"Well, you may be five hours ahead of us in time, but we are fifty years ahead of you in everything else."

The English subject was forced to pay for the cigars.

In 1583, while the Smithfield men were being prosecuted in a mild way, Edward, the head of the family to which the poet's mother belonged, was seized on a trumped-up charge of conspiracy against the Queen's life, and after a trial that was the talk of the country and also of foreign courts, was executed at Smithfield, the whole matter being arranged by Leicester, the Queen's favorite, who had reasons for hating Edward Arden, but Sir Thomas Lucy also took a part in the prosecution, and it seems quite likely these troubles might have led to Shakespeare's suddenly leaving home, perhaps after an outburst against Sir Thomas Lucy.

Whether the poet went to London, or whether he traveled in the provinces with the actors, whom he may have at first joined, has not been recorded. Of his life in London but little is known. Between 1585 and 1592, there is only one record concerning him, which shows that in 1589 he joined with his father in bringing a bill of complaint for the recovery of his mother's land from a relative to whom it had been mortgaged. In 1597, so great had been Shakespeare's success in London he was able to return to Stratford and purchase the most

Interior of Holy Trinity Church, Stratford-on-Avon, England.
Shakespeare's grave is in front of the altar, to the left.

important private house in the town, known as New Place. For this house, with its gardens and orchard, he paid the small sum of sixty pounds, or about $300.

In 1601 his father, John Shakespeare, was laid to rest in the old parish church and the year following the poet bought 107 acres of land. In 1605 he bought a portion of the local tithes and in 1607 his eldest daughter, Susanna, was married to Dr. John Hall, and in the year following the poet was able to attend the baptism of his first grandchild. For the next ten years matters went smoothly and in January 1616, the poet must have felt his end approaching, for he made his will, and on April 23, the anniversary of his birth, Shakespeare passed away, and two days following, April 25, was buried in the Church of Holy Trinity.

His widow, who will always be remembered as Anne Hathaway, rather than Mistress Shakespeare, lived until August, 1623, and on the 8th of that month was buried beside her husband.

A tour of Stratford-on-Avon is most interesting, the first place to visit being that of Shakespeare's birthplace, well known from its innumerable pictorial representations. Here is shown the very room in which the poet was born, the house in which the Shakespeare family lived, and the adjoining workshops in which his father, John Shakespeare, carried on the glover's trade. This house belongs to the town corporation, and is in charge of custodians, who give the particulars of the numerous objects here preserved. A portion of the building is set apart for what is known as the Shakespeare Museum, containing many relics of the great poet. This property was bought in 1847 by the corporation of Stratford. The main room of the house is the first one entered by visitors. At one time it was used as a butcher's shop and the massive chimney with its ample space for smoking hams and bacons, is the most interesting part. The living room behind this one has a similar great fireplace, with room for seats in the ingle-nook. Behind it again is a tiny parlor and the passageway leads to the back door, opening into the garden. From this living room a stairway goes down to the cellar and another up to a tiny landing off which opens the birth room of Shakespeare, over the main room. This bedroom has a similar great chimney. Its windows still contain a few of the old panes of glass, scratched all over with the names of notabilities. Across the little passageway, behind the birth room is what is known as the portrait room, from the fact that it contains the Stratford picture of Shakespeare. This picture has a curious history. It hung from an unknown date in a house belonging to the Clopton family and was bought from them by William Hunt in 1758. With the house certain pictures and fixtures were bought, but it was one hundred years later, in 1860, that some one suggested that the particular picture in question had been painted at two periods and that the latter work was very inferior to the original. When the latter work had been removed the picture appeared as it is seen today, and from its similarity to portraits of the poet was claimed as an undoubted Shakespeare. The room was originally divided into two apartments. The portrait is treasured in a large safe and is open in the daytime to visitors. In the rear of the house is a beautiful garden and a part of the property. Entering the main room again, and turning to the left, we have what is known as the Museum, containing a great number of most interesting exhibits of Shakespeare and his time. In addition to this is what is known as the librarian's room, with a great collection of pictures, rare prints, books, etc. Here is also Shakespeare's chair, from the Bidford Falcon, which is sat upon by almost all visitors, and here is also shown a letter written by Richard Quincy to Shakespeare, in 1598, asking a loan of thirty pounds. This is the only letter addressed to the great poet known to exist.

"I say," said the Captain, as we were walking towards the Anne Hathaway Cottage, "where are you going across those fields?"

"To visit Anne Hathaway's Cottage," I returned.

"Anne Hathaway," remarked the Captain, "Anne Hathaway; who is she?"

And then, of course, I informed him that she was Shakespeare's wife.

"Shakespeare's wife," remarked the Captain. "What was the matter with her?"

"Matter," I replied, "what do you mean by that?"

"What did they get a divorce for?" was the Captain's reply.

"Divorce," I remarked. "They were not divorced. Why do you ask this question?"

"Well," said the Captain, "if they were not divorced, why is she called Anne Hathaway? Why not Anne Shakespeare?"

And amid the summer's sun, I plucked a blade of grass and wondered where we were at.

The next most interesting place is the Anne Hathaway cottage which is located in Shottery, about a mile's walk across the fields and is a pleasant ramble at any time when the weather is fine. The Hathaway cottage has the strongest possible claim to the honor which has been accorded to it from time immemorial. Through the centuries the tradition had been verbally preserved that Shakespeare's wife was Anne Hathaway, and this was her home; and the confirmation given by the recently discovered marriage bond, with the name Latinized as Annam Hathwey, was very satisfactory.

The house is a good thatched farmhouse of the days of Queen Bess, divided late in the eighteenth century into two, and still later into three habitations. At the time I visited this place it was inhabited by a Mrs. Baker, a charming old lady, who has been for many years a custodian of this place. She was in her eighty-fifth year, and is descended from the Hathaways. The interior is interesting. The living room contains small latticed windows and a great open fireplace and a wooden settee, which it is said that Shakespeare and his wife used for courting. Passing up a flight of stairs we come to Anne Hathaway's bedroom, with its great four-posted bed. Strange to say, only two days before my visit, Ellen Terry, who has taken such an active part in Shakespeare's play, made her first visit to this cottage.

Along Henley street, at the top of the bridge, and at the corner of Wood street, is a curious little brick building, erected in 1810. Down the center of this street, until about 1860, stood Middle Row, a number of houses and shops dividing the street into two miserable, narrow thoroughfares. On the right is High street, and at the corner is Judith Shakespeare's house, the home of Shakespeare's younger daughter during the first thirty-six years of her married life. The house in question is owned by the corporation of Stratford. Immediately opposite the house and near the other side of High street, stood the market cross. Passing along High street there are curious glimpses up some of the narrow side alleys, and those who step within will find evidence that many of the houses now fronted with brick or stucco, are fine timbered buildings. The finest of them all, fortunately, retains its old carved fronts, and is well worth notice, known

Room in Which Shakespeare Was Born, Stratford-on-Avon, England.

as the Harvard House. Here, until her marriage in 1605, lived Catherine Rogers, who became the wife of Robert Harvard, and the mother of John Harvard, who emigrated to America and founded Harvard University, Cambridge, Mass.

At the other side of High street is the Shakespeare Hotel, full of mementos of the Garrick Celebration, of which it was the headquarters. Adjoining and a part of this establishment is the house of the five gables, the most picturesque piece of half timbered domestic architecture in the town. After crossing the bridge we come to the Memorial theatre, library and picture gallery, and just beyond is the Holy Trinity Church which Shakespeare used to attend and where the remains of both himself and wife are laid.

Holy Trinity Church, dating back to 1337, over 550 years ago, is an interesting place to visit. Edward III. gave this church a charter in 1413 and portions of the present church probably date from the time of the Conquest or thereabouts, when they were erected on the site of an earlier Saxon church. On entering this venerable house of worship we find the visitors' collection boxes, and a small pamphlet issued by the vicar as a guide to the church.

In a glass top box under the west window of the north aisle is the old parish register, open at the entries of the baptism and burial of Shakespeare. Here, too, is the chained Bible, and under the west window of the south aisle is the old font in which the poet was baptized. The church sets in about 300 feet from the road and is reached by a wide pathway lined with shade trees.

The Memorial theatre, library and picture gallery was opened to the public on April 23, 1879. The library contains some 7000 volumes, including the plays in a great number of editions and languages, books on Shakespeare and his works, plays of sixteenth century authors, books on contemporary history, costume, etc., and biographies of Shakespearean actors. In the center of the town is to be seen a fine memorial fountain, erected by the late George W. Childs, of Philadelphia.

There are many pleasant walks and drives from Stratford. Kenilworth and Warwick castles can be reached by an hour's drive through a beautiful country. There is a large number of stores in Stratford-on-Avon, devoted exclusively to the sale of curiosities and "Shakesperean mementos." While I was visiting one of these shops I was

Anne Hathaway's Cottage, Shottery, Near Stratford-on-Avon, England.

interested in an American lady who was bargaining for a genuine "Shakespearean plate," or, in other words, a plate that had been used by Shakespeare in his own family during his lifetime. The price of the plate was £1 or $5, and with it went a "certificate" from the shopkeeper to the effect that the article was genuine. The lady finally bought the plate, paying the price of the same. I afterward learned that about 200 of these plates are sold annually, and each one is guaranteed genuine, having been used by Shakespeare in his own family.

The Red Horse Tavern, of which mention was made at the commencement of this chapter, is located on the main street and is a quaint old tavern, entered through an archway to a sort of courtyard, or what we might call a stable yard. The entrance to the office of the tavern is on the left, and, strange to say, the office is nothing more nor less than a bar room, presided over by a barmaid. The first room on the left is called the Washington Irving Room. It is small, only 10x12 feet. Here Washington Irving made his home while at Stratford. In this room a portion of his "Sketches" were written. In a glass case is to be seen the identical chair which he used and also the old poker with which he used to stir the grate fire. There is also an old grandfather's clock here, which in Irving's day was used as a timepiece for the hotel. The walls of this room are lined with pictures and photographs of actors, actresses and notabilities, most of whom have visited Stratford-on-Avon and made this hotel their home.

It was toward the close of the afternoon of our first day at Stratford-on-Avon, when the Captain was looking a little weary, and turning to me remarked:

"How long do you expect to stay in this town?"

"A couple of days," I answered, "will be sufficient for us to see it thoroughly."

"Two days," said the Captain, "two days! What do you want to stay here that long for? Old Shakespeare is dead and we might as well get out."

I drowned my sorrows with an English cigar, and if the reader ever smoked one he can realize my sufferings.

CHAPTER XIX.

Chester and Hawarden.

AFTER locating in our hotel at Chester, one of the first things the Captain wanted to do was to take a carriage drive.

"Come," he remarked to me, "let's go out and see what we can 'charter' a hack for."

And I immediately followed my companion, until we were approached by a driver with a landau, when the following conversation between the Captain and the driver ensued:

"Say," remarked the Captain, "how much are you going to charge us for a couple of hours' drive around town?"

The driver eyed the Captain for an instant, sized him up from head to foot, and then remarked:

"Twenty-five shillings is the price, guv'ner—"

"I would not think of paying such a rate."

"As I was saying, guv'ner, twenty-five shillings is the price, but under the circumstances, I would take you for twenty shillings—"

"No, sir, I will not pay twenty shillings."

"But, as I was saying, while I would take twenty shillings, I suppose, under the circumstances, I would accept sixteen shillings—"

"Now, look here," said the Captain, "we do not propose to be buncoed by any rooster on this side of the Atlantic."

"While I would take sixteen shillings, still, if you object to the price, I suppose I might call it twelve shillings—"

The Captain turned to me and quietly suggested that we move on, when the cab driver once more approached my friend.

"If twelve shillings is too much, guv'ner, I will call it just an even ten shillings."

And on this basis the carriage was hired.

Upon our return to the hotel, the Captain remarked to me that he thought that if he had held out he might have hired it for six shillings, but he insisted that I kept interrupting him and that my presence with him on this occasion had actually cost him the difference between six and ten shillings or, in other words, one dollar.

The most ancient and antique city in all Great Britain is Chester, which is about three-quarters of an hour's ride from Liverpool. The city is beautifully situated on an elevated bank of the River Dee, and dates its origin back to the time when the Romans predominated in Great Britain. The city is completely surrounded by a wall, two miles in circuit, which at the present time is used for a promenade, and from which a fine view can be obtained. In times past many remains of Roman antiquities have been dug up in the vicinity of Chester. One of these, a crypt, is located under the establishment of Roberts & Co., Watergate street, wine merchants, and is used by them as a wine cellar. The date of the crypt is about 1180. Another may be seen under the establishment of Syrton & Grooms. The town is really a novelty from the fact that its houses are angular looking, with sidewalks for foot passengers on their roofs. These are covered with galleries for the purpose of protecting the promenaders from the rain. At the cross streets one has to descend and ascend each time. The road or street is sunk several feet below the level. Everything points to the fact that Chester was a city of no small importance as far back as the Middle Ages. History shows that with the fall of the Roman Empire, the Roman occupation of Britain came to a close. After the departure of the legions the entire country once more fell into a state of semi-barbarism.

Chester was a coveted spot, as it seems to have been in turn occupied by the Roman-Britons, the Saxons and the Danes, the latter retaining occupation only for a brief period, for Chester was restored to the Saxons by the valiant Ethelfleda, daughter of Alfred the Great, as far back as 971. Edgar occupied Chester with his victorious army, and his fleet filled the river in the vicinity of the city. In 1255 the Welsh, under their prince, Llewellyn, made an irruption into this neighborhood, carrying fire and sword to the very gates of the city. The year following, Prince Edward, who had recently been created Earl of Chester, paid a visit to the city, and received in the castle the homage of the nobles of Chester and part of Wales. The historical connections of the city are indeed interesting, dating back many years, and would make a volume. Considering the long occupation of Chester by the Romans, it is natural to expect that many

important remains of their public works should exist even to the present day. In the museum and other places are to be seen interesting relics of the past.

While crossing from Liverpool to New York, there were quite a number of people who were seasick. It interested the Captain to some extent, for he had never seen anyone in this condition before. It happened, however, he got in conversation with a doctor and asked him what was the cause of seasickness.

"Seasickness is a disease of the nerves," answered the doctor, "and is generally caused by the nervous system being out of order."

The Captain looked at the doctor for a moment and then replied:

"Well, I'll be hanged if I ever knew a person's nerves were in their stomach."

The doctor struck me for a box of cigars.

The most interesting place to visit in the city is the main business thoroughfare, where will be found the elevated sidewalks as described above and from which shops and stores of all description lead. Grosvenor park is an interesting place to visit and contains about twenty acres. A walk around the city walls of about two miles shows many places of historical interest and from this a very fine view of the city can be obtained. These walls are the most perfect of anything of their kind that I came across in my entire tour of England. Passing along above the Corn Exchange and to the left, so close that the sounds of its noble organ reach the ear, stands the grand old cathedral of St. Werburgh. Seen from this point on the walls, it is viewed to better advantage than from any other possible point in sight. The general plan and disposition of the cathedral are clearly to be made out. It is, like the generality of English cathedrals, a cruciform structure, comprising a nave, choir and transepts, with a massive tower rising at the crossing. Still further on we come to what was once known as Newton's Tower, at the present time called Phœnix. It is now a sort of small museum. On the door is inscribed a tablet with this announcement, "King Charles stood on this tower September 24, 1645, and saw his army defeated on Rowton Moor." It is said that the date is a mistake, as the battle actually took place on September 27, instead of September 24. The Roodeye or Roodee, near the Water Tower, is an interesting place and a curious legend is told of the spot, which may be given for the benefit of such as have a taste for old world tales.

Water Tower and Walls, Chester, England.

While making the walk of the wall of old Chester the Captain was much interested in the same, but I could tell by his nervous condition that he was either looking for or expecting something, and presently turning to me, he said :

"How far have we got to continue this walk?"

"It is two miles around the old city walls," I replied.

"How far have we gone?" asked the Captain.

"About one mile," was my reply.

"When are we going to see 'em?" asked the Captain.

"See whom?" I replied.

"Why, the Romans?" was the answer.

"What Romans?" I asked.

"Didn't you tell me before we came to Chester that the place belonged to the Romans, and here I have come all this distance expecting to see them."

Then, as I leaned over the wall, I was undecided whether to drop into the river Dee or go to the top of the Water Tower and end my existence from that point.

The story goes that ' Once upon a time the Christians of Hawarden, a few miles down the river, were in a sad strait for lack of rain. Now, it so happened that in the church of that place there stood a cross and image of the Virgin Mary, called Holy Rood. To her shrine then repaired the faithful and fearful of all classes to pray for rain. Among the rest Lady Trawst, the wife of the governor of Hawarden, prayed so heartily and so long, that the image, grown desperate we suppose, fell down upon the lady and killed her. Mad with rage at this ill answer to their prayers, a jury of the inhabitants was summoned, and the Holy Rood summarily convicted of wilful murder and other heinous sins. Fearful, however, of the consequence if they executed the offender, the jury determined to lay her upon the beach at low water, whence the next tide carried her away to the spot where she was found, under the walls of Chester. The citizens held a post-mortem examination, and seeing that she was Holy Rood, decided on burying her where she was found, and erected over her a simple stone cross, which, tradition says, we fear this time not very truthfully, once bore an inscription to the following effect :

> "The Jews their God did crucify ;
> The Hardeners theirs did drown,
> Because their wants she'd not supply,
> And she lies under this cold stone."

While returning home on the steamer Majestic the Captain was much interested in knowing the number of people that this great ocean liner was capable of carrying, and made inquiries of one of the officers, and was informed she had facilities for carrying 1800 souls, all told.

"In case of accident," remarked the Captain, "how are you prepared?"

"We have boats that will take off 1400 people," was the reply.

The Captain thought for a moment, and then added:

"I suppose the other 400 would be obliged to swim."

And if I had not been taught better in my early days I would have gone down and joined one of the poker parties.

Crossing over the bridge again a fine view is obtained of the Dee Mills, a massive pile of gloomy buildings, resting on the southwest end of the old bridge. The Dee Mills existed on this very spot shortly after the Norman Conquest, and were for centuries a source of immense revenue to their owners, the Earls. The reader, will, no doubt, remember the poem, "The Miller of the Dee," which had its origin here. Probably the finest salmon that are caught in England are from Chester, and the River Dee furnishes the source of supply. This is quite a fishing center and it has become quite an industry in this section. Passing along eastward, the visitor comes to what is known as the Light Suspension Bridge, erected in 1852. The steps from here which descend from the walls to the river side at this point are known as the "Recorder Steps."

It is most interesting to pass along what is known as the "Rows," or elevated sidewalks, of which it is almost impossible to trace the origin. Some writers attribute it to the Britons, while others to the time of the Romans. There are many interesting places to visit in Chester, including the Old Cathedral and numerous public buildings, which it would be impossible to describe here.

After we got ready to leave our hotel at Chester, the Captain was handed his bill and he repaired to the smoking room to look it over. During this time I was busily engaged in reading a newspaper, and the Captain seemed to be a little nervous. I noticed that he got up and left the room several times, going into the office and returning again. Presently he beckoned for me to come over and sit near him, which I did.

"Look here!" said the Captain. "My bill is all right except one item and I have been trying my best to make it out."

I asked him what it was and the item in question read as follows: "Boots, 2s," which translated into United States English, meant the services of a bootblack, fifty cents.

"What do you suppose they mean by charging me with boots, two shillings?" asked the Captain.

"Well," was my reply, "I guess it is correct. Why do you find fault with it?"

"Look here," said the Captain. "Did you ever know me to buy a pair of fifty cent boots? If I wanted to buy a pair of shoes over here, I would be willing to pay a decent price for them."

When I had explained to the Captain that his bill was correct and what it was for, he informed me that the next time he bought a package of cigarettes he would ask me to smoke one.

The richest man in all England is said to be the Duke of Westminster, and there is no question but what he owns one of the finest estates in Great Britain, known as Eaton Hall and located in Chester. This palatial mansion with its grounds is open to the public; a nominal admission fee of 1s, or twenty-five cents, is charged for admission to the residence, and this amount is donated by His Grace to charitable purposes in Chester. Eaton Hall is reached by either boat or carriage drive. The park is entered through Overleigh Lodge gates, and from there to the residence is a drive of about three miles through a magnificent park.

The family name of the Duke of Westminster is Grosvenor, which is one of the old families of this section. Eaton Hall, as it stands today, is the fourth mansion of the family. The present buildings were commenced in 1867 by His Grace, and were completed some years afterwards. Arriving at Eaton Hall the grand courtyard would probably first occupy the direct attention of the visitor. It is enclosed by fine iron work of the seventeenth century workmanship, while the entrance known as the Golden Gates, which belong to the hall, as it stood in the end of the seventeenth century, is flanked by modern iron work, made to accord in style. From the Golden Gates extend a noble avenue of trees, called the Belgrave drive, about two miles long. In the courtyard is to be seen the colossal equestrian statue of Hugh Lupus, the nephew and valued friend of William the Conqueror and one of the ancestors of the Duke of Westminster.

Eaton Hall, Chester, England.

The next place of interest is the stables, which are well worth a visit. They are fitted up in the most perfect manner, regardless of expense. In the center of the stable yard is a fine work by the late Sir J. E. Boehm, R. A., representing a rearing horse, held by a groom. On the other side of the yard is the chapel and lofty clock tower; the latter is 175 feet high. The interior of Eaton Hall is magnificent throughout.

The first place we enter in the family mansion is known as Central Hall, which is used on state occasions as a sort of reception room; from this we enter the grand salon, the ante drawing room, the drawing room, and the library, all of which are decorated with magnificent paintings, statues, etc., by the most famous artists. From here we pass to the grand corridor, where are two magnificent large oil paintings, one, "The Fathers of the Church," and the other, "The Adoration of the Magi," both by Rubens; the latter faces the grand staircase. Passing from here we go to the ante dining room, which from an architectural standpoint is not especially worthy of notice; nevertheless, it is almost equal to a grand hall. From here we enter the main dining room, decorated with six fine paintings, which adorn the walls, all by masters. The gardens and conservatories are planned on a large scale and mainly extend between the eastern facade of the hall and the River Dee. The main feature, directly opposite the hall, is a noble terrace, 400 feet in length, and from this the gardens descend to the river.

"This is an old town, isn't it?" I remarked to the Captain.

"Right you are," was his reply; "this is an old town."

"And an interesting one, too," I added.

"Interesting!" replied the Captain; "I don't know what you call interesting. This town is five hundred years behind the times. I haven't seen a single electric car, not a quick lunch counter, or a horseless carriage since I have been in the place. Talk about your interesting towns—"

And with that the Captain thought he spied a bag of peanuts in a store near by and made a dive for it, but unfortunately, and much to his disappointment, it turned out to be something else.

"Are you going to Hawarden?" remarked a gentleman whom I met at the hotel where I was staying in Chester.

"Hawarden," I answered, "where is Hawarden?"

Rt. Hon. William E. Gladstone.

His latest and best picture. At the right is his little granddaughter, who happened to put in an appearance when this was taken, and unknown to Mr. Gladstone.

"Only about six miles' drive from the very spot where you stand," was his reply.

I little thought I was within so short a distance of Wales, and the home of that grand old man, William E. Gladstone. Procuring a carriage we drove through a beautiful section of Chester and about a mile and a half from our starting point we came to the dividing line between England and Wales. The drive from Chester to Hawarden Castle was made in about one hour.

This is an old town and dates back to the early centuries. In 1337 Hawarden passed into the hands of the Earl of Salisbury and reverting to the Crown, was granted to the Duke of Clarence, second son of Henry IV. In 1454 it was made over to Sir Thomas Stanley, afterward Lord Stanley, whose son became the first Earl of Derby. Hawarden remained in the Stanley family for over 200 years. In 1653 it was purchased by Sargeant, afterwards Chief Justice, Glynn. At the Restoration a determined effort was made to recover Hawarden for the Stanley family and a debate took place on the question in the House of Lords. The purchase, however, was confirmed and Hawarden remained in the Glynn family until the death of the last baronet, Sir Stephen Glynn, in 1874. The lordship of the manor then passed by a family arrangement to Mr. Gladstone's eldest son. Twice Hawarden has been visited by English sovereigns. In 1495 King Henry VII. stayed there ostensibly for stag hunting, and Charles, when a fugitive, took refuge here in 1645. This, of course, was in the old or ancient castle, of which mention will be made later on.

Arriving at the outer gate or lodge of the castle grounds, a drive of about ten miles through a lovely grove and what might be termed a natural park, brings us to what is known as the Modern Castle, and as much as the Old Castle may interest the architectural visitor, the general visitor will find his interest centered in the modern one, the residence of Mr. Gladstone. The Modern Castle was originally a red brick, square house of no considerable size. This was built toward the middle of the eighteenth century by Sir John Glynn, who left Oxfordshire, where he had hitherto resided, and lived at Hawarden. Subsequently at different dates additions were made. The brick walls were faced with the stone of the district; additional wings were added, four turrets built, and the entire building was castellated. The whole work was carried out with a certain unity of design which has rendered the architecture pleasing, though unusual.

Hawarden Castle, the Gladstone Residence.

The interior, as usually happens in the case of country houses which have been added to at different periods, is roomy and comfortable. In the last twenty-three years three additions have been made. Mr. Gladstone's home is not in any sense a "show house" and it has been found absolutely necessary to adhere to a rule against the admission of strangers on account of the great number of applications received. The rooms are spacious and numerous, but they are not on the scale of the great country houses, nor are the pictures and objects of art sufficient to form an attraction in themselves.

Probably the most interesting apartment in the mansion may be said to be Mr. Gladstone's study, or as that gentleman appropriately terms it, "The Temple of Peace." Herewith is presented an illustration, which is an excellent one, of the exterior of Hawarden Castle; also a photograph of Mr. Gladstone himself, being the latest and most accurate one taken. In this photograph, at the right, will be noticed his little granddaughter, who happened to appear on the scene just as the photograph was being taken. There is also shown herewith an illustration of the "Keep," which is a part of the ruins of the old castle at Hawarden, and adjoins that of the new or modern castle.

The ancient castle of Hawarden is placed on a somewhat lofty eminence, on the south side of which is a deep ravine, which formed a great protection to the cast'e on that side. The exact date of the erection of this castle is undecided, but it seems almost certain it was founded during the reign of Henry III. and probably added to and completed in the reign of Edward I.

At the back of the old castle is a narrow entrance called Leopold's door, commemorating a visit in 1819 of the late King of the Belgians.

The leading points of the history of the castle may be very briefly touched upon. In the year 1264 it was the scene of the memorable conference between Simon de Montfort, Earl of Leicester, and Llywelyn, Prince of North Wales, in which the compact of mutual support and co-operation was entered into. The result of this was that the King, who was the Earl's prisoner, was forced to renounce his rights and claims and Llywelyn became possessor of the castle. On the collapse of Simon de Montfort's rebellion, the castle was claimed by the Crown and Llywelyn called upon to surrender it. There was, however, a fight over the old castle for many years, but the matter was

"The Keep." Ruins of the Old Castle at Hawarden.

finally settled. The Keep, or donjon, of the castle, as shown in the illustration above mentioned, is circular, sixty-one feet in diameter. At its base the walls are about fifteen feet thick, whilst it is tapered to about thirteen feet at the rampart line. It is an interesting old place to visit, and is open on certain days of the week to the public on payment of a small fee.

Hawarden Park comprises about two hundred and fifty acres and is a fine old estate. Driving in at the right one can make a tour of the place and come out in front of what is known as the old Hawarden village and the parish church, where the Gladstone family attend service. Just inside the park is the walk used by Mr. and Mrs. Gladstone, about one mile and a quarter in length, over which they pass from their residence to their church every morning. This church is supposed to have been built in 1275, and has much solidity and dignity of structure. The rector is Rev. S. E. Gladstone, who is a son of Mr. Gladstone. He has a staff of six curates, and has the responsibility of five additional churches and school chapels. Until recently Mr. Gladstone read the lessons every morning in the church, but within the past year has given up this work.

After finishing our tour of Hawarden, and upon returning home, the Captain turned to me and remarked that he was well satisfied with his morning's trip.

"Yes," I remarked, "it is very interesting to visit the home of Mr. Gladstone."

"Yes," said the Captain, "you are right. I suppose he has done more for mankind and womankind than any other living person."

This remark rather puzzled me for an instant, and fearing that the Captain might be laboring under a misapprehension, I asked him what he referred to.

"Why," was his reply, "to Gladstone's invention."

"To his invention," I replied, "what did Gladstone invent?"

"Why he is the man that got up the Gladstone bag," said the Captain, as he actually sneered at me.

And just at this moment the horses reared up, and the driver could hardly control them, but I sat calmly in the carriage, not caring much whether we ever reached our destination.

From Hawarden the drive was made back to Chester, and late in the afternoon we took the train for Liverpool, where we were to embark for home.

It was a beautiful September morning, the gray dawn was just visible, yet the lights from the distant shores were distinguished, as the good ship Majestic pulled off Sandy Hook. The Captain and myself were early on deck. We had been roaming foreign shores for four months, and we longed for a glimpse of our own native land.

"Look yonder, Captain," I remarked. "You see those lights in the distance?"

"Yes," was the reply.

"That is New York," I added, and just then the Captain glanced upward and saw the emblem of the greatest nation on earth floating in the autumn breezes.

"Hats off," shouted the Captain, as he uncovered his head.

"What for?" I asked.

"To the Star Spangled Banner," was his reply. And two Yankees stood on the deck of the steamer that early morn with their heads uncovered.

www.ingramcontent.com/pod-product-compliance
Lightning Source LLC
Chambersburg PA
CBHW032104220426
43664CB00008B/1129